THE 5 THINGS YOU NEED
TO KNOW ABOUT STATISTICS

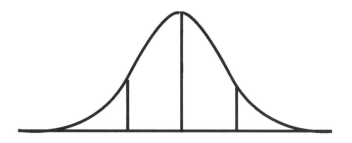

For Kathy

THE 5 THINGS YOU NEED TO KNOW ABOUT STATISTICS

QUANTIFICATION IN ETHNOGRAPHIC RESEARCH

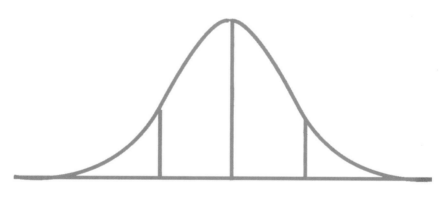

WILLIAM W. DRESSLER

LEFT COAST PRESS, INC.
WALNUT CREEK, CALIFORNIA

LEFT COAST PRESS, INC.
1630 North Main Street, #400
Walnut Creek, CA 94596
www.LCoastPress.com

ISBN 978-1-61132-392-4 hardback
ISBN 978-1-61132-393-1 paperback
ISBN 978-1-61132-742-7 consumer eBook

Library of Congress Cataloging-in-Publication Data:

Dressler, William W.
 The 5 things you need to know about statistics : quantification in ethnographic research / William W. Dressler.
     pages cm
 Includes bibliographical references and index.
 ISBN 978-1-61132-392-4 (hardback)—
 ISBN 978-1-61132-393-1 (paperback)—
 ISBN 978-1-61132-742-7 (consumer ebook)—
  1. Anthropology—Statistical methods. 2. Anthropology—Methodology. 3. Ethnology—Research. I. Title. II. Title: The 5 things you need to know about statistics.
 GN34.3.S7D74 2015
 301.01—dc23

Printed in the United States of America

∞ ™ The paper used in this publication meets the minimum requirements of American National Standard for Information Sciences—Permanence of Paper for Printed Library Materials, ANSI/NISO Z39.48–1992.

CONTENTS

ILLUSTRATIONS

Figures

Tables

ACKNOWLEDGMENTS

My interest in research methods in anthropology, and especially the mix of qualitative and quantitative methods, began with my undergraduate major in anthropology at Grinnell College. We had a methods seminar required in our junior year that was taught by Doug Caulkins. Doug had studied at Cornell and overlapped briefly there with Pertti J. ("Bert") Pelto. Bert was developing his own methods course that eventually would result in the book *Anthropological Research: The Structure of Inquiry* (1970). Doug used that book in our undergraduate seminar. Then, fast-forward a couple of years, when I was studying anthropology as a graduate student at the University of Missouri–Columbia. I took methods there from Mike Robbins, who had been Bert's student at Minnesota (and Doug and Mike had been undergraduates together at Carlton College), and again we used Bert's book. Well, it seemed only fitting that I should go to the University of Connecticut to do my Ph.D. with Bert, where I took his methods seminar for essentially the third time. So, to Doug, Mike, and Bert, I owe a great deal in formulating my thinking about methods in anthropology.

Along the way I took a number of statistics courses, including from the economist Jim Hamilton at Grinnell and the sociologist Ken Hadden at Connecticut, but none was better than the two-semester sequence I took at Missouri entitled "Multivariate Research Design in Anthropology" from Bob Benfer. At the time, I didn't realize how much Bob was shaping my thinking in quantitative methods. Bob is a remarkable anthropologist. He's the only person I know to have published primary research in all four subfields of anthropology. Over the years I have come to appreciate more and more his vision and to realize how lucky I was to have studied under him.

When I first arrived at Alabama I taught in a community medicine department in the medical school, and I became a friend and colleague of the biostatistician Jim Leeper. Jim was always open to me walking into his office, plopping down in a chair, and asking any and all questions. Jim is a widely respected statistician (having chaired sections of both the American Statistical Association and the American Public Health Association), and he is renowned as a teacher at Alabama, recipient of all sorts of teaching awards and in constant demand as a consultant and graduate committee member. I have been extremely fortunate to have drawn on his expertise.

Throughout my career I've been a part of a network of anthropologists interested in research methods, and it's hard to minimize how much all of these people have influenced my thinking. There are many of these colleagues, but I must single out Russ Bernard, Jim Bindon, Jim Boster, Doug Caulkins, Roy D'Andrade, François Dengah, Ted Graves, Lance Gravlee, Peter Guarnaccia, Penn Handwerker, Jeff Johnson, Kim Romney, Jay Schensul, Steve Schensul, and Sue Weller. I owe them all my thanks for helping me to understand issues of theory and method more clearly.

I also owe a debt of gratitude to my students, including those who have taken my methods seminars here at Alabama, those who have attended workshops I have participated in at the annual meetings of both the American Anthropological Association and the Society for Applied Anthropology, and those who took the short course in survey research methods taught under the auspices of the National Science Foundation. All of these students and their penetrating and insightful questions have required my rethinking of methods in anthropology.

The debt of gratitude that I owe to Kathy Oths, medical anthropologist, methodologist, ethnographer, editor, advisor, bonesetter, organic gardener, and the person I have the good fortune to be married to, is a debt that cannot be measured. Kathy puts up with a great deal from me, not the least of which is that I'm liable to launch into a discussion of research methods in anthropology anytime, anyplace, and she is always game for it. She has been my partner in teaching the workshops and short courses just noted, and she has been tireless as a colleague, commenting on, critiquing, and always improving my work. She has heard a lecture called "The 5 Things You Need to Know about Statistics . . . And the Rest Is Gravy" on numerous occasions. She has been encouraging me for years to write it up, and here it is, plus some additional thoughts.

I refer to much of my own research throughout this book, some of which was supported by research grants from the National Institutes of Health, the Pan American Health Organization, and especially by three research grants over a period of 20 years from the National Science Foundation (BNS-9020786, BCS-0091903, and BCS-1026429). I particularly want to thank Stu Plattner and Deb Winslow of the NSF Cultural Anthropology Program for their help and advice over the years. Also, I have carried out research in

Brazil in collaboration with my longtime colleagues José Ernesto Dos Santos and Mauro Campos Balieiro. Neither started out as an ethnographer, but both became enthusiastic practitioners of mixed-methods research, and I have always benefited from their insight and counsel.

While I was preparing this book, Muzel Chen of the Alabama Digital Humanities Center provided enormous assistance in finalizing the graphics, for which I will be eternally grateful. Finally, my thanks to Mitch Allen and his folks at Left Coast Press, Inc., including Jennifer Collier, Jack Meinhardt, and Ryan Harris, for guiding me through the production process and for their patience and encouragement.

William W. Dressler
February 2015

INTRODUCTION

With respect to research methods, anthropology is best known for ethno-graphic research, and other areas of study (including social work, nursing, and education, to name only a few) have adopted all or parts of that approach. Conveniently dated by the appearance of Malinowski's (1961/1922) classic ethnographies of the Trobriand Islands, the ideal of research is long-term residence in a community in order to learn as much about life as possible from the perspective of the members of that community. Ethnography is a process of discovery, to see the world as others see it. The methods on which ethnography is traditionally based are participant-observation and key-informant interviewing, although anthropologists have always used a mix of methods to collect data, and sometimes those data have been amenable to statistical analysis. The aim of this book is to help researchers to improve the quality of their fieldwork through better integration of qualitative and quantitative methods. This goal is dependent on grasping the basic logic of statistical analysis, and especially of how quantitative methods become an integral part of the overall configuration of methods employed in doing ethnographic research.

This book is about statistical thinking, to borrow Phillips's (1981) phrase, and not about statistics per se. It is not as odd for an anthropologist to write a book about statistical thinking as it might seem at first glance. As Moore (2012: 34) notes, the father of American anthropology, Franz Boas, taught a seminar in statistical methods throughout his entire career at Columbia University. From its inception, the method of cross-cultural survey research made use of available statistical methods. In the renaissance of research methods in the late 1960s and early 1970s, the call was made to integrate qualitative methods and quantitative methods in ethnography, in order to improve the validity and reliability of ethnographic data (Naroll & Cohen 1973; Pelto 1970; Pelto & Pelto 1978).

More recently, a figure no less prominent in contemporary theory than Pierre Bourdieu (1984) relied on social survey data and the multivariate statistical technique of correspondence analysis to elucidate patterns of taste that convey social distinction in France. Russ Bernard (2011) has been tireless in his promotion of what is now call mixed-methods research—or what anthropologists 40 years ago called the quantitative-qualitative mix—in order to expand the tool kit for ethnographers. And there are anthropologists—including at least, but not exclusively, Kim Romney and Sue Weller (Romney, Weller, & Batchelder 1986; Weller & Romney 1988)—who have made fundamental contributions to the development of numeric methods of analysis.

I hasten to point out that I do not include myself among these brilliant and pioneering methodologists. I am a user of statistical techniques, not an innovator. Whatever virtue my work has lies in connecting the dots, from theory to fieldwork to measurement to analysis and conclusion. I use and borrow, in order to better do the work that I do. And ever since the first research methods course I took as a junior in college, I have been convinced that integrating qualitative and quantitative methods leads to a more refined examination of our hypotheses. Traditional statistical methods allow the ethnographer to subject his or her insights in the field to more stringent evaluation, simply because to do so one must take into account the way in which phenomena are distributed (Pelto & Pelto 1975). A purely qualitative approach can also take into account the distribution of phenomena, and it should. With traditional statistical methods, however, one can eliminate at least the alternative hypothesis of chance occurrence, and, with more sophisticated techniques, one can eliminate all sorts of alternative explanations in whatever area one is studying.

To do so requires a certain style of thinking: statistical thinking. It is a cognitive style that is powerful and systematic, and one that must be cultivated. It doesn't come naturally (or, at least it didn't come naturally to me). But neither is it all that difficult. The problem is that the big picture of statistical thinking can get lost in the detail and minutiae of statistics itself. In a way, you can think about it as though it were a bit like an anthropological perspective. Understanding the nuance of culture, and specifically the way in which one's culture of orientation creates a multifaceted lens through which everything is refracted, is a powerful perspective, yet subtle at the same time.

My major professor in my doctoral program, Pertti J. ("Bert") Pelto, sometimes opined that we don't really teach anthropology; rather, as a student, you just have to hang around and be exposed to it long enough for it to seep in and start to make sense. And of course you have to do ethnographic research.

Thinking statistically is a little like finally learning to think anthropologically: it changes forever the way you see things. In my experience, however, students in anthropology and related social sciences can be severely put off by statistics before they get to the point of being able to think statistically.

Why? Like any field, statistics has its own lexicon, which can be formidable. There is also a certain math anxiety that can afflict those who are drawn to the social sciences by the beauty and mystery of human cultural differences. Finally, there is the simple fact that so often we end up taking our statistics courses from sociologists, economists, psychologists, and biostatisticians, all of whom I respect and admire. The problem is that they don't tend to talk about anthropological or ethnographic stuff. When you are talking about the correlation coefficient, and its application is being illustrated by the association of the different rates of sales tax and the number of cartons of cigarettes sold in municipalities across the United States (can you guess that I took my first statistics course from an economist?), you can start to wonder: what am I going to do with this?

Buried under an exotic language, conveyed via complicated formulae, and embedded in unfamiliar examples, is *thinking statistically*.

I have been teaching statistics off and on for about 40 years. Mostly I do not teach introductory statistics, usually for reasons of time and efficiency; there are so many introductory courses in statistics available in any given university, it seems like a waste of resources to offer yet another one. My students will normally have taken their introductory course somewhere else. They then arrive in my seminar on multivariate and mixed-methods research. I think that they are ready to dive right into multiple regression analysis. The problem is, they often don't seem to have grasped the basic underlying logic of statistical analysis. They come in knowing t-tests, and the chi-square, and correlations, yet they don't seem to get what these statistical tests are really good for and what they are really telling us. And don't get me wrong, I am not faulting students' professors. Far from it. Perhaps I am faulting the culture of the teaching of statistics, since every time I look at syllabi for introductory statistics courses, they look like they came from exactly the same master template for teaching statistics.

So, I developed an introductory lecture in which I tried to convey what I regard as the elemental features, the building blocks, of statistical thinking. Sometimes the lecture is given in 90 minutes, sometimes in three hours, sometimes all day, depending on the setting. Mostly it has been presented to graduate students in anthropology, although I have also used it with full-fledged anthropologists and other social scientists taking research methods workshops. Over the years a number of students and colleagues have encouraged me to expand and publish this lecture as a short book. This is it.

One day, just for fun, I called this lecture "The 5 Things You Need to Know about Statistics . . . And the Rest Is Gravy." "And the rest is gravy" is an antique phrase. An online database of American idioms and expressions (www.usingenglish.com/reference/idioms) defines it as follows: "If the rest is gravy, it is easy and straightforward once you have reached that stage." What I mean is that there are five things that you need to know about traditional approaches to statistical inference that, in my opinion, if you grasp them, enable you to understand most of what else you may wish to learn.

When I say "grasp," I don't mean that you have memorized enough to be able to get an A on your statistics final (although that's a good thing, too). What I mean is having a real gut-level, intuitive sense of the meaning of these five things. I really don't care, for example, if you can't remember the formula for the standard deviation. Nor is it particularly important if you get wrong the proportion of cases that fall between one standard deviation above and one standard deviation below the mean. What I do care about is your having a gut-level feeling for what the standard deviation means and what it enables you to do in thinking about a sample of people (or potsherds or whatever). I believe that grasping these five points will do two things. First, it will enable you immediately to graduate to mixed-methods research in your own fieldwork. Second, it will provide the cognitive foundation for about 99% of what most of us need to do in elaborating our mixed-methods approaches. The rest, indeed, is gravy.

What are these five things?

- Measures of central tendency in a sample, especially the arithmetic mean.
- Measures of dispersion in a sample, especially the standard deviation.

- The logic of statistical significance testing using the chi-square.
- The logic of statistical significance testing using the analysis of variance.
- The correlation coefficient.

Understanding—really understanding—the logic of inference using this way of approaching data will provide the background you need to go on and do whatever you want in numeric analysis (with more study, of course!).

The 5 things you need to know about statistics makes up the first half of this book. The second half is an extended meditation on integrating quantitative analyses into the larger ethnographic research enterprise. When you start to "do" statistics, you frequently run into people who are certainly more highly trained and more adept at statistics than you are. Not surprisingly, they begin to level a critique at your use of statistics that comes out of more purely quantitative fields such as survey sociology and epidemiology, as though you are merely trying to tack the same things they do onto what you do. One of my major points here is that, in doing mixed-methods research in anthropology, this mere accretion of methods is emphatically what we are *not* doing. Rather, we are reorganizing the ethnographic enterprise so that participant-observation, key-informant interviewing, cultural domain analysis, and the collection and analysis of quantitative data coalesce in a novel configuration or functional organization, the aim of which is to answer questions of social scientific interest. And, I argue, one of the main questions of interest, especially in anthropology, is how people's local cultural construction of their immediate experience locates them in a space of shared meaning, which in turn can have profound influences on people's behavior, perhaps even more profound than those influences posited by purely etic theory. This, I argue, is a major point of integrating qualitative and quantitative methods and data in ethnographic research.

I tend, obviously, to think about these questions in terms of my own research in medical anthropology from a biocultural perspective. As I have argued elsewhere, integrating this ethnographic enterprise with traditional anthropological interests in phenomena such as biological plasticity offers a rich opportunity for a better understanding of human biological variation (Dressler 1995, 2005). And I think that this fundamental ethnographic perspective can be useful in a variety of fields.

SOME PRELIMINARY CONSIDERATIONS

This book is about the 5 things you need to know about statistics, but, of course, some preliminary considerations are necessary before one applies statistical thinking. The most important of these is that you have to have some data! Methods books in anthropology, and especially Bernard's (2011) excellent guide, provide a comprehensive overview of data collection for both qualitative and quantitative analysis. I am not going to try to be in any way comprehensive in a discussion of data collection here; however, statistical thinking starts with thinking about data collection.

All data, whether qualitative, quantitative, or somewhere in between, come in the form of a *matrix*. A matrix is an array of anything in the form of rows and columns. If you buy a local newspaper in any medium-size community and flip to the entertainment section, you'll find the television listing for the day in the form of a matrix. In my local newspaper the rows represent the TV channels, with the old broadcast networks in the first five rows and cable channels in the subsequent rows (usually limited to whatever channels are provided by basic service from the local cable companies). Columns represent time periods, and in our daily paper just the evening times are listed, from 6:00 P.M. to midnight, in 1-hour gradations. So, you have an array of time versus TV channel, and there are cells in the matrix created by the intersection of time and channel. On a Sunday night, you go to the column that is the 8:00 P.M. hour, follow that column down to the Public Broadcasting Service, and you find that Masterpiece Theater is in that cell. A matrix is an efficient array for organizing information.

Doing fieldwork and collecting data qualitatively generate the same kind of matrix, although, in our discussions of fieldwork, we do not often talk about these results as forming a matrix. Imagine that you are doing fieldwork regarding treatment choice in a community. You are working in a community in which there are a variety of different sources of health care that can be sought in response to illness, and you want to find out how people decide to go where they go. So you interview 10 respondents (or what traditionally are called *informants* in anthropology, despite the questionable connotations of that term). You start by asking "When was the last time you were ill?" After determining how the illness was labeled and what the symptoms were, you follow up by asking what the respondent did in response to the illness. Did she treat it herself? Did she have something in the house already to treat the illness? Did that resolve the problem? Did she have to visit a healer? What kind of healer did she visit? And so on.

Once these open-ended interviews have been recorded and transcribed, the work of sifting through them to find themes begins. Perhaps in reading the transcripts you might distinguish between illnesses that are short term and relatively limited versus longer-term illnesses that might be considered chronic. Then, there may be a theme dealing with what medications are kept in the home and which are shared by friends and family and which are purchased from a market or a pharmacy. The point is that once you have gone through this exercise—known as "coding"—you will end up with an array of data in which your 10 respondents are the rows and the themes that you identify are the columns. Then, in each intersection of row and column you have words, the portion of your respondent's narrative that applies to a given theme. Your analysis of these data will consist, in part, of finding similarities and differences among your respondents in their descriptions of the illness episode and of seeing if differences in the way they deal with an illness (for example, do they self-treat or go to a healer?) is associated with other features of the illness (for instance, is it short term or long term?). You are, in short, looking for patterns, and the data matrix facilitates that process.

Data for quantitative analysis are arrayed in the same way, with one fundamental difference: for quantitative data, numbers are assigned to categories. To provide a very simple illustration linked to the example just given, in a study of treatment choice using qualitative analysis, you might discover a theme regarding the alternative sources of treatment employed for a single illness episode. Perhaps an individual self-treats, then seeks advice from a pharmacist, then goes to a primary-care physician, who refers him to a gastroenterologist. In your qualitative analysis, you describe this process in the words of the respondent. But you might decide that you want to quantify this description as "number of treatments employed," which in this case would obviously be 4. You have just assigned a number to a category.

This is the process of measurement. In a quantitative study, you have a matrix of rows and columns, and where they intersect there is a number. In somewhat more technical terms, your columns have now become "variables," because the rows of the matrix, your "cases," vary in terms of those characteristics. In general, this is *research*. We select a sample of cases, often referred to in statistics as the objects of study, and we make a series of observations on those objects that distinguish between them. The question becomes: why are all these objects so different in terms of the variables?

Numbers and the variables they describe come in several different forms. In traditional approaches to teaching statistics, these forms are introduced as **nominal, ordinal, interval,** and **ratio,** according to Stevens's (1946) classic typology of measurement level. I like to simplify this a bit at the outset by distinguishing between **categorical** and **continuous** variables. In this simplified typology, categorical variables are nominal variables, whereas interval and ratio variables are continuous variables. Ordinal variables occupy somewhat of a middle ground. At times an ordinal variable can be so simple that we regard it as merely assigning people to one set of categories. At other times, however, ordinal variables can approximate true continuous variables.

A categorical variable is just that; it assigns an individual case to one category or another. When there are just two categories, such as "male" or "female," we speak of it as a *dichotomy.* You either are or aren't (in most cases, this works for gender, although not always). Other kinds of variables require more categories (for example, religious affiliation, political party, and so on). But there is no inherent order among the categories. You are just in one and not in the other (or the rest).

Some ordinal variables are much like categorical variables, except that there is a sense of order among the categories. This order can be very, very simple, as when I might ask you if you are "not at all," "somewhat," or "very" happy. In general English language usage, being somewhat happy is usually being happier than being not at all happy but not as happy as being very happy. How much more or less? Who knows? All we know is that it is more or less. Still, though, there are just three categories that describe this order. This is one example of an ordinal variable, and here it resembles a categorical variable.

However, if I ask you how tall you are (people are actually pretty good at reporting their heights), and you respond that you are 6 feet tall, I know for sure that if I stacked two of the end-tables in my house, each of which is 3 feet tall, on top of one another, the top of the top table would be pretty much even with the top of your head. (Why I might do this, other than to satisfy my curiosity, is another matter.) Also, I know that if you walked into my kitchen and I had moved the breakfast table, you would bonk your forehead on the lighting fixture, since I have 8-feet ceilings and the lighting fixture hangs down 28 inches (which is why I have a breakfast table under it—I'm 6 feet tall myself).

How do I know all this? Because we measure height in feet and inches, and each inch is an equal interval (hence the term interval measurement). Unlike the difference between being "somewhat" and "very" happy, which we know is different but we don't know by how much, since every inch is the same interval, we know that putting two 3-feet-high objects together is going to equal a 6-feet object. And we know that a 6-feet tall object is likely to come into contact with an object that is 5 feet and 8 inches off the ground. If I knew only that you were taller than a breadbox but shorter than a giraffe, I couldn't come to such a precise conclusion. Measures in inches (and feet) are made up of equal intervals that order cases along a continuum, and so we can be much surer of the actual distance between the cases on that continuum. The last type of continuous measurement, the ratio level, has the added proviso of a true zero point (which, if you think about it, height probably does not have).

It also turns out that an ordinal measure that has lots of gradations on it, even if we don't know absolutely for sure that those gradations are equal intervals, can fairly precisely order cases along a continuum. For example, in a few pages I introduce a measure that has different values that we can use to order people from lower to higher on the measure. We don't however, have any idea if, like inches, the distance described by each gradation is the same. In the very strict sense of things, this would still be an ordinal variable, but an ordinal measure that has many gradations actually begins to act like a continuous variable. We should not lull ourselves into a false sense of security thinking that it has equal intervals; nevertheless, it can act an awful lot as though it does have equal intervals, which enhances our ability to use more sensitive statistical analyses. We just have to be careful, in the end, that we remember what that measure is really doing, which is ordering cases. Both categorical and continuous measures are very useful. Continuous measures can really be useful, especially those of the equal interval type, given the precision with which we can distinguish among cases.

Much of the time, but not always, we divide our variables into different sets, depending on the role that they play in our theory. Some variables are thought to exert influences on other variables, the latter thought of as the result of the former. Here we are talking about **independent variables**—the causes—and **dependent variables**—the results. There are some analyses in which we are not so much interested in thinking about causal pathways as we are in thinking about the patterns or configurations of association among variables, at which point the independent-dependent distinction becomes less useful. There are also variables that we want to introduce into the analysis just so we don't have to think about them; that is, they are associated with variables of interest, but they don't interest us for themselves. These are **covariates, or control variables.** (Age in years is an example of a variable that often gets introduced into analyses in order to remove what might be a confounding effect; this situation is discussed in some detail in Chapter 7.) But remember that these are distinctions we make in our theories, because one person's control variable might turn out to be another person's independent variable.

A SAMPLE SET OF DATA

Statistics books usually have lots of examples. In this book about statistical thinking, I'm going to go with basically one example. I think this approach is useful because it allows us to become much more familiar with a set of data, which I hope will enable you to think through the various examples more thoroughly. I have been working in Brazil for about 30 years, with a research focus on social and cultural factors associated with health. This research has been carried out in the city of Ribeirão Preto, the third largest municipality (population approximately 600,000 people) in the state of São Paulo, in the north of the state near the border with Minas Gerais (see Dressler, Balieiro, & Dos Santos 1997, 1998, 2015; Dressler, Balieiro, Ribeiro, & Dos Santos 2005, 2007b; Dressler, Oths, Ribeiro, Balieiro, & Dos Santos 2012).

Working in Brazil requires that one pay careful attention to the potential role of social inequality. One way of doing this in Brazil is to interview people with different levels of completed education, because educational level is strongly associated with economic status. My colleagues in my Brazil work and I have employed this approach mostly in gathering qualitative data. In our survey work, to collect quantitative data, we have concentrated on four neighborhoods that differ in economic status. We collect data from random samples of individuals and households selected within each of these four neighborhoods (for what statisticians call a *stratified sample*, neighborhoods representing the strata; see Dressler & Oths [2014] for a more thorough discussion of sampling in anthropological fieldwork).

A general hypothesis guiding our research is that the more closely an individual can approximate in his or her own beliefs and behaviors the prototypes for belief and behavior encoded in shared **cultural models**—or what I refer to as **cultural consonance**—the better his or her health status (Dressler 2007a). (I introduce a measure of cultural consonance in Chapter 5.) In examining this hypothesis, my colleagues and I have used a variety of other variables as alternative explanations, covariates (or variables for which we want to control), and as outcome variables. One of these is *health locus of control*. The concept of locus of control is an old one in the social sciences, associated specifically with the psychologist Julian Rotter (1990). It's a straightforward notion: sometimes I feel like my behavior is something that I have initiated, that it is completely under my control. Other times I feel as though I've ended up doing something that I didn't necessarily choose or even want to do but that I was compelled to do by forces outside my control. In the first case, I can be described as having more of an *internal locus of control*: the control of my behavior is within me. In the second case, I can be described as having more of an *external locus of control:* my behavior is controlled by forces external to me. If there tend to be more instances in which I feel that my behavior is under my control, then I might be said to possess the trait of an internal locus of control. If there are more instances in which I feel that my behavior is under the control of external forces, then I might be said to possess the trait of an external locus of control.

Some years ago, Coreil and Marshall (1982) introduced a short scale of health locus of control (abbreviated as HLOC). We adapted the 14 items for the scale as follows:

1. Thinking of illnesses, what happens will happen.
2. Sometimes I feel like I'm being "pushed" in life.
3. There are things I can do to change some important things in my life.
4. Most diseases will improve, no matter what treatment was used.
5. When people get sick, it is usually not by chance.
6. For many of the problems I have, I have solutions.
7. When people get sick, one should ask God for help or they will not improve.
8. If God wants to send a disease to you, there's nothing you can do.
9. There are many things I can do about things that happen to me.
10. When someone gets sick, you can usually do something to help him get better.
11. If you get sick, it's because you are living under extreme pressure.

12. When I have a problem, I think carefully about it.
13. I always feel able to deal with my problems.
14. People who have good health are the lucky people.

For about half of these items (1, 2, 4, 7, 8, 11, and 14) the sense expressed by the item is that there is nothing one can do about things, especially illness, that happen in life. For the other items the sense expressed is that one can take charge and change one's life. Respondents were asked to agree or disagree with each statement. (Note that having items phrased in different ways helps to avoid what are called **response sets**, or just saying "yes" or "no" to every question.)

If a person agreed with items 3, 5, 6, 9, 10, 12, and 13, and you and I wanted to code in the direction of an internal locus of control, we could give her one point for each time she agreed with the statement. Then, for items 1, 2, 4, 7, 8, 11, and 14, we could give her one point for each time she disagreed with the statement, because that again would be consistent with an internal locus of control (that is, she is rejecting the notion of external forces being more important).

Doing this, we would have a scale that, at least hypothetically, could vary from 0, in which an individual gives no answer consistent with an internal locus of control, to a score of 14, in which an individual answers every question in a way consistent with an internal locus of control. We would have a continuous measure that ordered people along a continuum of increasing internal locus of control. My Brazilian collaborators and I did just this in 1991, and then again in 2001 and 2011, in Ribeirão Preto. In 1991 we did it just as I have described, simply asking people to agree or disagree. Later we expanded the responses available to people so that they could express the degree to which they agreed or disagreed with the statements. For the sake of simplicity, you and I are going to work with the 1991 scale throughout this book, because of the intuitive appeal of the responses (that is, a scale score indicates the number of questions on which a person responded in the internal locus of control direction).

Why are we even justified in thinking that we can combine these responses in this way? Is there any reason to think that there really is this psychological continuum out there that varies from a very external to a very internal sense of control in life? This is a complicated question that depends both on theory and data for an answer. But considerations of the theory of locus of control would take us too far afield; for now we can just agree that it's a reasonable notion. From a data standpoint, it turns out that people reliably respond in one direction or the other; that is, if you tend to answer a subset of questions in the external locus of control direction, then you tend to answer other questions in that direction, too. Similarly, if you tend to answer some subset of questions in the internal locus of control direction, then you tend to answer other questions in that direction, too. There is, in other words, an **internal consistency** (meaning a consistency within the scale) to how people respond to the questions, which tends to indicate that it is a useful way to order people.

My colleagues and I have published analyses using this scale elsewhere (Dressler, Balieiro, & Dos Santos 1998, 2002). Here, I am going to use a subset of those data to illustrate my discussion. These data come from a random subsample of 100 persons drawn from the 1991 study in Ribeirão Preto. You can download these data from the following site: go.lcoastpress. com/dressler, either as an SPSS data set or as an Excel spreadsheet. I have made these data available so that you can use them in a statistical package and experiment with the statistics that I present in this book. Regarding statistical packages: throughout the book I illustrate what I am doing with statistical routines and output from the Statistical Package for the Social Sciences, better known as SPSS. I do so not out of any particular allegiance to SPSS but because it is what I have used for most of my professional life and because it is relatively commonly encountered on college campuses. Furthermore, there is a freeware clone of SPSS (called PSPP) that is available that allows you to do many of the things that I talk about in this book. So if you wanted to you could download PSPP right now, download the data, and work through many (though not all, since this program is still under development) of the examples as I present them.

There are, of course, plenty of other statistical packages out there, including SAS, STATA, Minitab, SYSTAT, ANTHROPAC, and, for the particularly code-savvy among you, the freeware R (and see especially Simple R). Fortunately, in this day and age, everything does pretty much the same thing. Forgive me for veering off into a bit of curmudgeonly nostalgia, but I wrote my dissertation in the late 1970s, when all we had was the classic mainframe, the IBM370. We entered our program commands and data on punch cards, fed them (along with everyone else in the university) into the mainframe via a card reader, and then waited anywhere from an hour to overnight to get our hardcopy printout back. If we made a single mistake in a program command, we started over. Also, back then, the commercial appeal of statistical analysis programs had not become apparent, so basically university computing centers wrote their own packages and made them available to other schools. The code for SPSS was originally written at the National Opinion Research Center at the University of Chicago (using taxpayers' dollars, I suspect). Then there was BMD and BMDP from UCLA, P-STAT from Princeton, Osiris from Michigan, and several others. Each of these programs did slightly different things, reflecting the data analytic predilections of their authors (SPSS came from survey sociologists, BMD from biostatisticians, Osiris from psychologists, and so on). When I was writing my dissertation, I had to use SPSS, BMDP, and Osiris, because there was no one package that included every statistical routine I needed to use.

Well, things have changed for the better in that all packages available are nearly comprehensive and they all run on laptops. My point in all of this is for you not to get too hung up on which package you use. They all work in very similar ways. The examples that I give from SPSS will be easily translatable into whatever program you choose to use.

SUMMARY

The aim of this book is to introduce the interested reader to a way of thinking statistically. I suggest that there are five basic concepts that lay the foundation for much of the way anthropologists and other social scientists use statistics and numerical inference in their research. These five basic concepts include the mean; the standard deviation; the logic of statistical significance testing using the chi-square; the logic of statistical significance testing using the analysis of variance; and the correlation coefficient. With a grasp of the logic that underlies each of these concepts, the interested reader will be in a position to go on and study statistics seriously, since much of what we do at an advanced level is based, in one way or another, on the ideas underlying these five statistics. The rest is, indeed, gravy.

Beyond the 5 things you need to know is the logic of incorporating quantitative methods and data into ethnographic research. I argue that there is a unique configuration of methods, from the purely qualitative to the purely quantitative, that characterizes ethnographic research. The strength of our work lies in that unique configuration.

SECTION I

The 5 Things You Need to Know about Statistics

Measures of Central Tendency: The Arithmetic Mean

This chapter introduces the first concept that must be absorbed in learning to think statistically: the central tendency, especially the arithmetic mean. As I said in the Introduction, in 1991 colleagues and I interviewed a sample of 271 people in the city of Ribeirão Preto, Brazil. It was in this study that I developed the concept of cultural consonance (Dressler 2007a), and we included the measure of HLOC, or health locus of control, that I described in the Introduction. For our exercises here, for the sake of simplicity, we are going to work with a random subsample of those data for 100 people (these data are available at go.lcoastpress.com/dressler to be downloaded as either an SPSS data set or an Excel spreadsheet so that you can do these analyses yourself).

As a first step in thinking about these data we want to understand how they are distributed across the sample. One way to do this is numerically, as illustrated by the Frequencies routine in SPSS. (To do this, go into the SPSS drop-down menu under "Analyze," select "Descriptive Statistics," and then select "Frequencies." Drop the HLOC variable into the "Variable(s)" window and click "OK.") These results are shown in Table 1.1. This table is itself a small matrix.

The rows of the matrix are formed by the various values that it is possible for the HLOC scale to have. There are 14 questions answered "yes" or "no"; hence there are 15 possible values (because someone can answer with either an internal or external locus of control response to each and every one of the questions). The first column of the table represents these values, 0 through 14. Then, the next column gives the number of people answering at that particular level on the scale. There is indeed one person who sees him- or herself as hopelessly buffeted by the world around him (or her). However,

---

TABLE 1.1 Frequency distribution of locus of control scale scores

		FREQUENCY	PERCENT	VALID PERCENT	CUMULATIVE PERCENT
	.00	1	1.0	1.0	1.0
	1.00	2	2.0	2.0	3.0
	2.00	3	3.0	3.0	6.0
	3.00	3	3.0	3.0	9.0
	4.00	5	5.0	5.0	14.0
	5.00	10	10.0	10.0	24.0
	6.00	8	8.0	8.0	32.0
VALID	7.00	11	11.0	11.0	43.0
	8.00	14	14.0	14.0	57.0
	9.00	13	13.0	13.0	70.0
	10.00	10	10.0	10.0	80.0
	11.00	7	7.0	7.0	87.0
	12.00	4	4.0	4.0	91.0
	13.00	7	7.0	7.0	98.0
	14.00	2	2.0	2.0	100.0
	Total	100	100.0	100.0	

there are two people who respond with the internal locus of control answer to every single question. They see themselves as totally in control of what happens to them. The other 97 people are arrayed between these extremes. The third and fourth columns of the table provide this frequency of response as a percentage of respondents who answer at that particular level. There are two different columns in the event that we have one or more persons who did not respond to one or more questions in the scale and hence have the dreaded missing data (note: try to avoid missing data if at all possible!). Happily we don't have any missing data, so the two columns are the same. Finally, we have a column of cumulative frequencies. A cumulative frequency is the proportion of respondents who have a particular score (such as 5) or lower (so the cumulative frequency at the score of 5 is 24%).

Numeric frequency tables like this one are great, but as anyone who has taken any course from me can tell you, I *really* like graphics. A common way of visually representing these data is called a *histogram*. You can get SPSS to output a histogram along with the frequency table, or you can separately go into "Graphs" and request the histogram. SPSS has become more sophisticated in recent years in enabling you to customize your graphs. Sloth often leads me within "Graphs" to "Legacy Dialogs," which is another way of saying that this is an old-fashioned way of doing things. Under "Legacy Dialogs" you select "Histogram" and put the variable HLOC into the "Variable" box and click "OK." The histogram for these data is shown in Figure 1.1. Along the horizontal axis of the figure we see arrayed the values for HLOC that represent, again, the number of questions to which individuals respond with an internal locus of control response. The vertical axis here represents the number of people at each level of response who answer that number of questions with the internal locus of control response. The bars are drawn with a height equal to the number of people answering that way. So here we see at level 0 a bar that is 1 unit high, because of that one person who did not give a single internal locus of control response. Then, at level 14 we see the two people who answered every single question with an internal locus of control response.

FIGURE 1.1 Histogram of locus of control scale scores

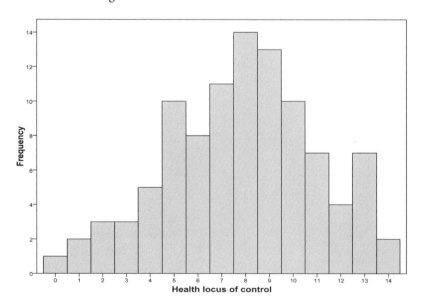

An interesting thing about this frequency distribution is that the more frequent responses occur in the middle, around 8–9; that is, there are more people who answer about half the questions with an internal locus of control response than there are people who answer either all or none of the questions that way. And from that most frequent middle, people tend to shade off in number in each direction.

OK. So, imagine that you and I are sitting in a coffee shop (or a bar; it depends on the time of day) in Ribeirão Preto, and my friend, João, comes by. He joins us, and just for fun I turn to you and ask: "So, what do you think João's level of internal locus of control is? I mean, what do you think he scores on the HLOC scale?" You sensibly reply: "Well, I have no idea. Why don't you ask him?" But I continue, and João plays along: "Come on! Guess!" What would you guess? You have no real idea. His level of locus of control could be anything, and you don't want to be too far off. So what would you guess?

It is likely that you would want to use the average of all the responses, or the **arithmetic mean**, as your guess. And it's the same, good-old, garden-variety mean you would use to calculate how much you spent on average per week on dog food during the last year:

EQUATION 1.1

$$(X_1 + X_2 + X_3 + X_4 + ... X_n)/n.$$

In this equation (and there won't be many of these in this book: I promise) each X represents the sum of a person's internal locus of control responses or his or her scale score on HLOC. The X with the subscript n just means that you add them all up for the number of people there are in your sample, or in this case 100. And then you divide by that total, again in this case 100.

The mean is 7.85. So you say to me, "7.85!" You have just turned into a statistical modeler, because there is no way that an individual could actually have an HLOC score of 7.85, since I don't know how anyone would answer 0.85 of a question. Rather, you are using a simple model—the mean—to represent something about this distribution and then using that representation as your answer.

It's actually a pretty good answer, which you can see graphically in Figure 1.2. I've placed an "x marks the spot" where the mean would fall in this

FIGURE 1.2 Histogram of locus of control scale scores, showing location
of the mean

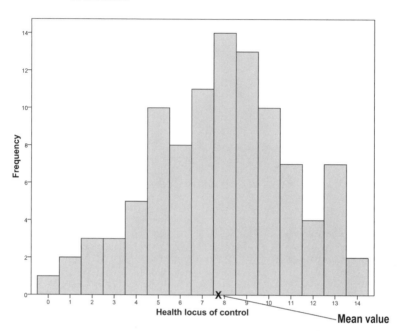

frequency distribution. And it looks good. It is sitting about in the middle
of the distribution of responses. You can almost imagine that the frequency
distribution would balance right on that spot.

It turns out that your guess is a good one in a more technical sense. In
Figure 1.3, I've had SPSS superimpose the normal distribution on top of the
histogram. The normal distribution describes the way a lot of things end
up getting distributed in nature. Lots and lots of distributions approximate
this bell-shaped curve (including, regrettably, the grades that students get
in my introductory anthropology course—I want all my students to get an
A, yet that inevitably fails to happen). Is HLOC distributed normally? No.
True normal distributions do not exist in nature, only in the minds of the
statistically minded. But, HLOC comes pretty close. There are too many
people with a score of 5 and not enough people with a score of 6 for it to be
a perfect curve. There are some other bumps and dips where there shouldn't
be, but all in all, it comes pretty darn close. Again, there are no normal
distributions in nature, only approximations of them. If our distributions
approximate a normal distribution, that's good enough.

FIGURE 1.3 Histogram of locus of control scale scores with superimposed
normal distribution

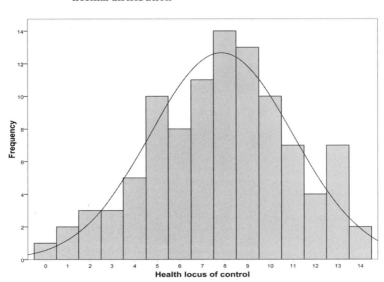

But back to why your guess is a good one. In a normal distribution, the mean or average has the happy property of coming closer to every value in the distribution than does any other number. No matter what else you guessed, you couldn't come any closer to every other value than you could with the mean or average.

So, you confidently respond to my challenge to guess João's level of locus of control with "7.85," knowing that you are coming closer to it than with any other guess.

You know, also, that you are likely to be wrong, and I don't mean in the trivial sense that nobody can answer 0.85 of a question. You could say, well, since the mean falls between 7 and 8, I'll guess "8," since that's close to the mean. But there are only 14 people with the HLOC scale value of 8, meaning that there are lots and lots of people who don't have that score. So you confidently respond with an answer of "8," knowing that you are more likely to be wrong than right.

And that's OK, because the issue is not that you are wrong in your guess, the issue is how wrong. Is there any way I can evaluate the *confidence* that I can have in my guess? This is the question of the dispersion of the distribution, and especially the calculation of the standard deviation, to be taken up in the next chapter.

SUMMARY

This chapter has been about thinking about your data as a distribution and specifically characterizing that distribution by its central tendency in the form of the arithmetic mean or average. I have urged you to think about that distribution in a particular way: guessing what a single individual's score might be in that distribution. Lots of statistical analysis is about trying to guess one thing from another (the highfalutin' term for that is *estimation*). And we start guessing with the mean, because lots of our variables approximate normal distributions, and the mean has such nice properties for those distributions.

A simple thing like a central tendency can get complicated fast. For example, another way of characterizing a distribution would be to find the value of your variable (HLOC in our case) that divides the sample into two equal parts. Then you would be right in the middle of the distribution. This is called the *median*. Another way of characterizing a distribution is called the *mode,* which is simply the most frequent score. The median and the mode are useful characterizations. In our sample, the mean, as we have seen, is 7.85, and the median is 8.0 and the mode is 8.0. This is another clue regarding the degree to which HLOC approximates a normal distribution. The more normal the distribution, the closer the mean, median, and mode. When those three measures of central tendency start to diverge, the distribution looks less and less like a bell curve.

There are actually good reasons why some distributions depart more from normality. For example, I've got another data set from Brazil with a scale of depressive symptoms in it. The mean for that distribution is 19.5, the median is 16, and the mode is 7. What that indicates is that there is a distribution that has a long right-hand "tail": there are a few people reporting rather high levels of depressive symptoms, and they drag the mean up (the tail of the distribution refers to the curve superimposed on top of the distribution and the way that at each end the curve goes down). The point dividing the scale into two groups is lower than that, and the point where "most" people pile up is lower still. Why does this distribution look this way? Think about it: would you want to live in a world where depressive symptoms are normally distributed?

But even the departure of a distribution from normality—what is called the **skewness** of the distribution—does not preclude treating it as if it were closer to normal, as long as it's not too skewed and as long as we keep our wits about us (that is, we know that we are doing it). Why would we want to do that? Well, we will see that the payoffs from being able to use the statistical techniques based on the normal distribution are large in terms of analytic strength, but, again, we need to be aware of what we are doing, so as not to say things we really ought not to say.

If we just can't treat the distribution of a variable as approximating normality, we need not despair—there are lots of other things we can do! But, again, that's the "gravy" part of this. What I want you to understand are the basics of statistical inference, and concentrating on variables that tend toward normality and taking advantage of that tendency are what we want to do right now.

Also, just for the sake of completeness, I have been emphasizing the use of the arithmetic mean. There are other ways of computing means (such as the "harmonic" mean and the "geometric" mean), but again, that's not our point here. Our point is to learn the basics, and the main point here is that the arithmetic mean is a good guess regarding somebody's score value in a distribution, even though you know you will almost certainly be wrong.

Measures of Dispersion: The Standard Deviation

We are still sitting in Ribeirão Preto with our friend João, and I have challenged you to guess his level of locus of control. You have figured out that a very good guess is the arithmetic mean of the distribution, since that number will come closer to every other number in the distribution. And, you know you are likely to be wrong. The question is: how wrong will you be?

This is an issue of confidence in a statement. We think in terms of the confidence that we can place in statements all the time. For example, you are sitting around with a group of friends listening to music, and you are all trying to figure out just when it was that Ronnie Wood joined The Rolling Stones. You say, "Well, I think it was in the mid-1970s. It certainly wasn't much earlier than about 1973, nor was it much later than 1978." (It was 1975, by the way.) Here you are offering an estimate (the mid-1970s), and you are trying to place a certain interval around it in which you have confidence (because you are saying it wasn't very much earlier nor very much later than your estimate of the mid-70s).

This is an everyday example of what statistically we refer to as a **confidence interval.** You are guessing at something, and you are trying to put some limits around that guess in which your confidence is higher (in other words, you are quite sure that Wood didn't join the Stones as early as the 1960s or as late as the 1980s). In statistics this can be done in a variety of ways, but the most basic, when you have a more or less normally distributed variable, is the **standard deviation.**

Basically what we want to know is how far away each person (or whatever it is you are studying) is from the central tendency, the mean:

The 5 Things You Need to Know about Statistics: Quantification in Ethnographic Research by William W. Dressler, 39–46 © 2015 Left Coast Press, Inc. All rights reserved.

EQUATION 2.1

$$\left(X_1 - M\right) + \left(X_2 - M\right) + \left(X_3 - M\right) + X_4 - M) + \ldots \left(X_n - M\right).$$

The standard notation for the mean in most statistics books is an X with a line over the top ($\bar{X}$), but M to denote the mean is also in use in some literature, so I'll adopt that here, because it is descriptive.

If you reflect on what would happen if you simply subtracted the mean from each observation, and then added up those deviations, the result would be zero. This again is a characteristic of a normal distribution. If people are evenly distributed around the mean, then if you subtract the mean from each observation, half of those numbers will be negative and half will be positive. Furthermore, assuming the distribution is truly balanced on the mean, for every negative number there will be a corresponding positive number. Hence, add them up and you get zero.

To make this somewhat more useful, we do the following:

EQUATION 2.2

$$\left(X_1 - M\right)^2 + \left(X_2 - M\right)^2 + \left(X_3 - M\right)^2 + \left(X_4 - M\right)^2 + \ldots \left(X_n - M\right)^2.$$

Squaring each of the difference terms will get rid of the negative numbers. Then, you divide by the number of people in the sample:

EQUATION 2.3

$$\left[\left(X_1 - M\right)^2 + \left(X_2 - M\right)^2 + \left(X_3 - M\right)^2 + \left(X_4 - M\right)^2 + \ldots \left(X_n - M\right)^2\right]/n.$$

And we have just calculated another average. Only this time we are calculating the average amount that each individual's score for his or her set of locus of control responses deviates from the average locus of control responses for the distribution. It's an average that includes an average. (You will sometimes see this calculated with $n - 1$ in the denominator, but don't worry about that. Right now the concept is more important.)

Technically, what we have here is called the **variance.** It is an extremely useful calculation in and of itself and gets used in lots of ways, but, for our purposes here, it is not so useful. All of that squaring to get rid of the negative numbers has the unhappy result of throwing off what the statistically minded call the **metric**. This is one of those cool-sounding words that really just refers to the original units used for the scores. In our case this metric is literally the number of questions to which a respondent gives an internal locus of control response. All the squaring has thrown off our ability to think about (or *interpret*) the number we just calculated: the variance, or the average amount, by which individual scores deviate from the overall average.

But we can get our original metric—our interpretable numbers—back:

EQUATION 2.4

$$\sqrt{[(X_1 - M)^2 + (X_2 - M)^2 + (X_3 - M)^2 + (X_4 - M)^2 + \dots (X_n - M)^2]/n.}$$

That's right. You square all those numbers, then "unsquare" (if that's a word) to get back to our original and interpretable numbers. We take the square root of the average deviations (or variance) and we get the standard deviation: 3.15. So, we have a distribution with a mean of 7.85 and a standard deviation of 3.15. There are a variety of ways to get the standard deviation in SPSS. If you have been working along with the examples, you will see that it is automatically printed out in the legend of the histogram. If you want to do it in "Frequencies," go to "Analyze," then to "Descriptive Statistics," and then click on "Frequencies." Put HLOC into the "Variable(s)" box and then click on "Statistics." Within "Statistics" you see that you can select a whole variety of stuff, but, for right now, just check the boxes associated with the "Mean," "Variance," and "Standard deviation" (which is abbreviated here as "Std. deviation."). Click "Continue" out of that drop-down menu and click "OK." Another way to do it is to go "Analyze," "Descriptive Statistics," and then "Descriptives." Put HLOC in the "Variable(s)" window and click "OK." This will automatically give you the mean and the standard deviation.

In the literature, you will sometimes see the mean and the standard deviation written as $M = 7.85$, $s.d. = 3.15$. Sometimes it will be $M = 7.85$, ± 3.15 (the mean "plus-or-minus" the standard deviation). And, sometimes it will be $\bar{x} = 7.85$, $\sigma = 3.15$ (the lowercase Greek letter sigma is sometimes used to represent the standard deviation).

So, what does this "plus-minus" business mean? Literally, it means that, typically, people in this sample respond to 7.85 of the 14 questions—or, more sensibly, about 8 of the questions—with internal locus of control responses. And, again typically, people in the sample deviate from that average by 3.15—

or, more sensibly, about 3—questions in which they answer with an internal locus of control response.

Let's go back to the histogram to look at this. In Figure 2.1, I have indicated the point on the spread of answers where 1 standard deviation below the mean would be and where 1 standard deviation above the mean would be (each indicated by an asterisk). Pause for a moment to consider the part of the distribution that is encompassed by how we have just bracketed it. The average number of internal locus of control responses is about 8, and on average either people are going to answer 3 questions fewer than that in terms of an internal locus of control response, or they are going to answer 3 questions more than that in terms of an internal locus of control response. Consider the number of people that fall in this interval (that is, look at the bar heights in between 1 standard deviation above or below the mean—this gives you a visualization of the number of people there). If the distribution approximates a normal distribution, then about ⅔ of the people (actually 68%, but 2/3 is easier to remember) will fall between 1 standard deviation below and 1 standard deviation above the mean.

FIGURE 2.1 Histogram of locus of control scale scores, indicating area of the distribution encompassed within 1 standard deviation below and above the mean

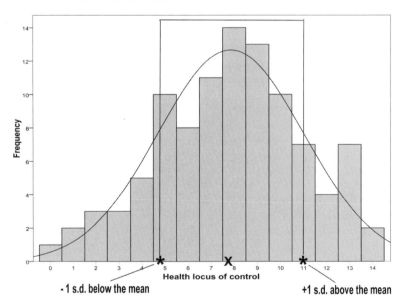

About ⅔ of the people in this sample are going to answer somewhere between 5 and 11 questions as an internal locus of control response. So, if I ask you to guess João's score on the HLOC scale, you can get very sophisticated in your answer. You can say: "Look, this is just a guess, but I would say he answered about 8 questions as an internal locus of control-type person, and I'm pretty sure that he answered somewhere between 5 and 11 questions that way. In fact, if you bring 10 of your friends here, I would guess that 6 to 7 of them would have HLOC scores between 5 and 11."

What you have just done is to place confidence intervals around your estimate of the HLOC score for João. Figure 2.2 shows the histogram for HLOC scores, only this time with 2 standard deviations below and 2 standard deviations above the mean indicated. In this case, you are bracketing 95% of the cases by taking into account 2 standard deviations either direction from the mean (and, you might note, that 7.85 plus 2 standard deviations is actually a number larger than the largest possible score in the sample—these things happen when you don't have perfectly normal distributions and/or you have

FIGURE 2.2 Histogram of locus of control scale scores, indicating area of the distribution encompassed within 2 standard deviations below and above the mean

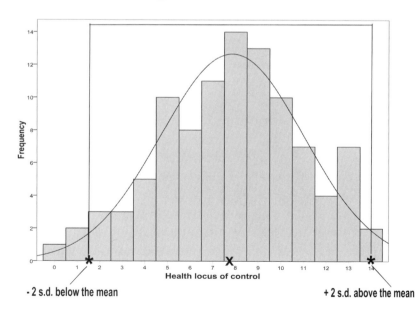

a pretty modest sample size). With 2 standard deviations taken into account, you can say that someone will tend to a score of 8 but that you are going to be right 96% of the time that their score will be between 2 and 14.

Considering that the scores range from 0 to 14, this is a little bit like saying that someone is going to win the Super Bowl this year. In other words, isn't this some kind of misplaced numerical precision that doesn't really help us to understand the world anthropologically? Aren't we just goofing off with numbers here, when we should be interpreting the world?

Granted, simple examples can seem to be pointless. But what is important to learn here is the basic principle of characterizing a distribution in terms of its central tendency and then in terms of how it is spread around that central tendency. This basic idea extends to thinking about all sorts of distributions.

While we are on the subject, let's go back to one of the original bits of arithmetic we used to calculate the standard deviation:

EQUATION 2.5

$$\left(X_1 - M\right)^2 + \left(X_2 - M\right)^2 + \left(X_3 - M\right)^2 + \left(X_4 - M\right)^2 + \ldots \left(X_n - M\right)^2.$$

Again, what we are doing here is subtracting the mean from each person's HLOC score, squaring the result (to get rid of the negative numbers), and adding it up. When you stop and think about it, this resulting number doesn't mean much of anything by itself, but it does represent the total amount of variation in the sample. Now this is not the total range of variation in the sample (we know that is 0 to 14). Rather, this is the total amount by which people vary *relative to the mean* in the sample. It will obviously differ from one sample to the next, even given relatively similar ways of collecting the data. But for any given sample, it captures how much variation exists in the way people are answering the questions.

In statistics, you run across the phrase "the sum of the squared deviations" a lot. This phrase refers to a process of summing the deviations (squared) of observations from some central point. In this case, we are talking about the sum of the squared deviations from the mean. In other cases we'll talk about the sum of the squared deviations from other kinds of calculated values. In general, it is very useful to think about variation in a sample relative to some value; the total amount of variation can be captured by summing up the deviations of individual values from whatever statistic—like the mean—we are interested in at that moment.

In this chapter we have focused on the standard deviation as a way of evaluating the dispersion in the distribution. There are other statistics for evaluating the dispersion. The overall range of the distribution—in this case from 0 to 14—is one such statistic. There is also what is called the **interquartile range**, which, as it sounds, is the range of scores that characterize the distance between the 25th percentile and the 75th percentile. In this sample the interquartile range is 6 to 10. These are all useful things to know.

The standard deviation is somewhat more useful, however, because characterizing the dispersion of distributions in this way will be used to describe a variety of different distributions. Another useful thing you can do with the standard deviation is to calculate what is called a *z-score*. A **z-score** is a way of converting each individual's score in the sample to a score that is relative to the central tendency and dispersion. The formula for calculating a *z*-score is $(X_n - M)/s.d.$ That is, you take each person's score, subtract the mean, and then divide by the standard deviation. The mean and the standard deviation characterize the whole sample. A *z*-score indicates where each individual in the sample sits in terms of the mean and standard deviation.

Take, as a simple example, someone whose score is very close to the mean, for example, 8. This person's *z*-score would be $(8 - 7.85)/3.15$, or 0.0476. Or, take someone whose score is 7. This person's *z*-score would be $(7 - 7.85)/3.15$, or $- 0.269$. We are converting people's HLOC scores to a new value that is *relative* to the mean. Imagine a person with an HLOC score of 11. His or her *z*-score would be $(11 - 7.85)/3.15$, or 1.0. Note that this person's HLOC score is actually 3.15 standard deviation units above the mean, or 1 standard deviation. In other words, by using the mean and the standard deviation, we are measuring an individual's distance from the central tendency in terms of a proportion of the standard deviation. Keep in mind that each person has his or her own *z*-score.

Since we are calculating a relative distance from the mean, and since some people are below the mean, a bunch of our *z*-scores (about half) are going to be negative numbers (note the previous example). What this situation signifies in terms of calculating a mean of the *z*-scores is that it is always going to be 0.0 (this result is intuitive when you think about the positive and negative numbers balancing each other out). Perhaps less intuitive, but nonetheless true, is the fact that the standard deviation of a distribution of z-scores is always going to be 1.0. And this fact is true no matter what the original units are—the mean will always be 0.0 and the standard deviation will be 1.0. Z-scores can be very useful in a variety of different situations. They can be so useful, in fact, that SPSS will output them for you automatically. If you use "Descriptives" under "Analyze"/"Descriptive statistics," you can check a box in the lower left-hand corner that will automatically output z-scores for each individual in the sample and add them to your data set.

SUMMARY

In this chapter we talked about the second of the five things you need to know about statistics, the dispersion of the distribution as assessed by the standard deviation. The most important point here is that it is this measure of dispersion that enables you to place confidence intervals around your guess (or "estimate"). In our lowly example of just trying to guess a mean, such "confidence" may not seem to have narrowed your range of error very much. But, again, I just want you to get the idea, because this idea will get extended to how we can place confidence in all sorts of estimates.

The Logic of Statistical Significance Testing: Chi-Square

At this point, sitting in Ribeirão Preto with João and me, you are probably starting to get a little irritated. You are thinking, quite rightly, that I am being unfair in expecting you to guess João's level of locus of control even though you know absolutely nothing else about him. Surely, you think to yourself, if I knew a little more about this guy, I could make a more educated guess.

You, of course, are correct, and you are beginning to think **bivariately**— that is, you want to find out something else about your respondent and use it to help predict his level of locus of control. So, what do you want to know? This is precisely the point at which theory becomes so valuable. Our theories lead us to think about how the world works. Theories describe processes that link one variable with another. So, I hope, you have been reading the literature, examining carefully what other researchers have chosen to study in their research on locus of control or similar kinds of variables, and you have steeped yourself in anthropological theory to help guide your selection of variables of focus.

One thing you might want to know about are economic circumstances. You reason that people who are somewhat more well off economically will have had life experience in which they are able to accomplish, more often and to a greater degree, what they set out to do, simply by virtue of their economic circumstances. They have been able to purchase the kinds of material goods they want. They have been able to more easily enter into certain kinds of social relationships, because they have the economic resources to support that participation. They therefore grow to understand that if they choose to do something, there is a reasonable probability that they will be able to do it. So, if you knew about João's economic circumstances, you could make a better guess. Maybe.

There are a whole variety of ways to characterize people's economic circumstances in Ribeirão Preto—for our purposes let's use neighborhood of residence. Other indicators of economic status, such as income and education, correspond very closely with neighborhood of residence in Ribeirão Preto. As I noted, we used a stratified sampling technique in our survey research with neighborhood of residence as the strata to capture socioeconomic variation, so let's use that here. Also, for even greater simplicity, I'm going to collapse our four neighborhoods into two categories: "lower socioeconomic status" and "higher socioeconomic status" (and I'll use the convention of SES to refer to socioeconomic status).

Also, to make this exercise more clear, I'm going to collapse HLOC into two categories, "low" and "high," which in this context essentially makes the low category equivalent conceptually to an external locus of control and makes the high category equivalent to an internal locus of control. Collapsing a measure from one level to another is noteworthy here. As a general rule, you can always "reduce" a more precise measurement to a simpler measurement. We break up continuous measures like this all the time, as when we decide to call blood pressure in excess of 140/90 mm Hg "hypertension," and blood pressure lower than that "normotension." Sometimes there are good reasons to do this, and sometimes we mistakenly choose to do it. You always have to stop and think about these sorts of decisions carefully, because you end up throwing away information. Also, unless you have a good reason for reducing measurement levels, you can end up either obscuring patterns in the data that could be detected with more sensitive statistics, or you can incidentally make it seem as if there are patterns there that actually aren't. I'll explain how this works later on. But for our purposes of exploring what you need to know about statistics, we are going to do it here.

It's not hard to break the neighborhoods into low and high SES, because there are only four of them. Returning to Table 1.1, however, we have to figure out how we want to break HLOC into two groups. The classic statistical answer to this question is to use the median. Why? Well, because the median gives you two groups of equal size, and that's a good thing. The median for these data, you recall, is 8, and looking at Table 1.1 we see that 8 doesn't exactly give us two groups. There are 57 people who have a score of 8 or below and thus 43 who have a score above 8. Welcome to the real world! As I said, there are no true normal distributions in nature, so we just have to do the best we can and divide the sample into two groups using that point in the scale.

One of the handy things about all statistical packages is that they enable you to change your variables in various ways, usually called "transformations." In SPSS, go to "Transform" and then to "Recode into Different Variables," which enables you to create two new variables, one for neighborhood coded into SES and one for HLOC coded into external versus internal. Note here that, in general, you should always keep a purely "raw" data set. By that I mean that you should always keep your data in the form in which you originally collected and coded it (and back it up about three different ways!). If you make any changes in the coding by hand, or you transform the variables in such a way that you lose the original coding, then you are stuck. You can't go back again. This doesn't mean that you can't transform and save transformations to generate a new "working" data set. Just never, ever lose that original set. So here, in "Recode into Different Variables," you put *bairro* (that's Portuguese for "neighborhood" and fits into the variable box nicely) into "Input Variable" window. Then rename it (I like to prefix my categorized variables with "cat," for obvious reasons), and then click "change," which will flip that new variable name—"CatBairro"—into the center window. Then click "Old and New Values"; this gives you a variety of options for how you want to make the changes. We start with the "Old Values," in order to tell SPSS where we are starting. In our example, the two less well-off neighborhoods are coded 1 and 2, so we can use the recoding process that gives us a range. We can click on the option for "Range" and put in "Range: 1 through 2." Then, in "New Values" we put a new code to represent both of those neighborhoods. I suggest that we give them the code of "0" (that's "zero"; in the long run you will find it very handy to code dichotomies as 0 [zero] and 1 [one]). When you have put in your new code, click "Apply" and go back and do this all over again for the more well-off neighborhoods, which are coded 3 and 4 in the original data and will be recoded as 1. After you have completed that, you click "Continue," which takes you back to the original Recode menu. Click "OK," and the new variable will be added to your data set. Then repeat this process to recode HLOC and create "CatHLOC."

So, for all 100 persons in our sample, we know two things: their neighborhood of residence (and hence their SES) and their locus of control orientation—external or internal. Using these two bits of information we are going to create what is called a *contingency table,* which is just a table that has two rows and two columns in this case (since each of our variables here are categories and, even more technically, **dichotomies**—there are only two categories). This contingency table is also sometimes called a **2 x 2 cross-tabulation,** because each variable has 2 categories, and each individual in the sample is being allocated to a new category based on where he or she falls in each of the categories of SES and HLOC. For each individual, we (actually, SPSS) place each person into the cell of the table that corresponds to her or his combined categories of SES and locus of control. To do this, go to "Analyze," then "Descriptive Statistics" and "Crosstabs." Put the variable CatBairro into the "Row" window, and put the variable CatHLOC into the "Columns" window. Then click "OK." This process results in Table 3.1. One thing you can do first is to look at the very ends of the rows and the very bottoms of the columns. In the language of contingency tables these are called **marginals,** or **marginal totals.** As you can see, they are just the number of cases that are classified as low or high SES, in the case of the rows (for example, there are 49 people with high SES and 51 people with low SES), and external (57 people) or internal (43 people) locus of control, in the case of the columns. These marginals are equivalent to the **univariate distributions** of these variables, since the variables are dichotomies.

In the cells of the table, we have the **bivariate distribution** of the variables, showing how persons get classified simultaneously in terms of two variables, in this case low or high SES and external or internal locus of control. Look first at the row of the table representing low SES: 38 of the 51 people who are low SES also report an external locus of control, while 13 of those 51 people report an internal locus of control. Now look at the second row of the table: 19 of the 49 people classified as high SES report an external locus of control, while 30 of those 49 people report an internal locus of control.

TABLE 3.1 Cross-tabulation of SES and locus of control

		LOCUS OF CONTROL		TOTAL
		External	*Internal*	
SES	*Low*	38	13	51
	High	19	30	49
	Total	57	43	100

Would you be tempted to conclude that, by knowing a person's SES, you could reduce your uncertainty in guessing his or her locus of control? That is a very tempting interpretation, because the tendency for low SES to go with an external orientation and high SES to go with an internal orientation is undeniable. But how confident would you be in drawing that conclusion?

This question of confidence is like our earlier question of confidence in guessing the mean. There are of course a variety of things that go into assessing confidence, including your trust in how good a job you did in selecting people to interview, your conviction that neighborhood of residence is a reasonable way to assess SES, and your belief in the validity of your measure of locus of control.

There is another issue of confidence: are you certain that the distribution of people you see in Table 3.1 isn't a matter of happenstance, the luck of the draw, a mere chance occurrence? After all, coincidence is real. Odd things happen all the time that cannot be explained on the basis of some underlying set of causal processes. Maybe the distribution of cases in Table 3.1 is a case of happenstance. (See Mlodinow [2009] for an entertaining discussion of just how much randomness is part of our daily lives.)

Here we are arriving at the essence of testing statistical significance. Although statistical significance testing is often enshrined in a strange language of null hypotheses, what this testing boils down to is: how easy would it be to see this pattern by sheer luck, having nothing to do with the influence of economic resources on psychological processes? This is the question that lies at the heart of all tests of statistical significance. Put another way, what we want to do is compare the results we have actually obtained with the results that we could anticipate if nothing but happenstance or luck was at work. Put less prosaically, what if chaos rules in the universe? You have put forth a hypothesis opposed to chaos. You are suggesting an orderly progression from experience in the world to psychological disposition. But what if no such orderliness prevails (at least in the realm of SES and locus of control)? How would your results—generated by your theoretical model—compare to a model of chance?

The beauty of contingency table analysis is that, unlike somewhat more complex forms of statistical analysis, it allows you to see the comparison with chance outcomes right before your very eyes. We have 100 persons in the sample. How would they be distributed if there was absolutely no relationship between SES and locus of control—if a person, no matter his or her experience in the world in terms of economic resources, was just as likely to end up in one category of locus of control or the other one? If you are thinking that there would be about 25 persons in each cell, you are right. I have put these numbers in parentheses in the cells of the table shown in Table 3.2. Technically, the marginals are thought of as "fixed"—these marginals are just the way that the dichotomous variables are univariately distributed in the population. Therefore, if we are guessing at how the cases will be distributed by chance, the first row should add up to 51 not 50, and the second should add up to 49 not 50, but bear with me. This is an example!

So now we have two sets of numbers: the number of persons by SES and HLOC that you collected and the numbers of persons by SES and HLOC that a model of a chaotic universe would predict. What can we do with these? Basically what we would like to know is how different the distribution of persons based on your actually collected data—which we will refer to as "observed" data—is from the distribution of persons that we would anticipate on the basis of pure chance—which we will refer to as "expected" data. Since we want to know how different they are, then it would make logical sense to calculate some differences. How about the following (and I'm squaring things to get rid of negative numbers)?

Difference 1 = (observed cases in cell 1 – expected cases in cell 1)^2

Difference 2 = (observed cases in cell 2 – expected cases in cell 2)^2

Difference 3 = (observed cases in cell 3 – expected cases in cell 3)^2

Difference 4 = (observed cases in cell 4 – expected cases in cell 4)^2

And, for good measure, let's calculate a sum:

Total difference = Difference 1 + Difference 2 + Difference 3 + Difference 4.

What will happen with the "total difference" as your observed data begin to resemble less and less the data anticipated on the basis of chance? Yes, the "total difference" will get bigger and bigger the more your results diverge from chance.

You might—indeed you should—object here that even weird outcomes can happen by chance, and you would be absolutely correct. Take, for example, flipping a coin. (I can almost hear the collective groan out there,

TABLE 3.2 Cross-tabulation of SES and locus of control, showing expected values based on equal distribution of cases

		LOCUS OF CONTROL		TOTAL
		External	*Internal*	
SES	Low	38 (25)	13(25)	51
	High	19 (25)	30 (25)	49
	Total	57	43	100

since people talking about statistics inevitably end up talking about coin flipping—bear with me, it's a very good way to introduce a certain topic.) I have reproduced a histogram of coin flipping in Figure 3.1. You probably know the drill here. Take a coin and flip it 20 times. Each of these 20 flips represents an instance, or "trial" as it is sometimes called. Then do that 1,000 times (yes, that means flipping the coin 20,000 times). For each of the 1,000 trials, you record the number of heads (and this particular figure shows the proportion of times you get each outcome—that is, you'll get exactly 10 heads and 10 tails about 18% of the time). You will not be shocked to observe that most of the time you get a .50/.50 split, or 10 heads (and hence 10 tails). Will you have instances when you don't get the .50/.50 split? Of course! That's the way the world works. Sometimes you will have 11 heads and 9 tails; sometimes you will have 8 heads and 12 tails. These things happen.

Will you have instances of 17 heads and 3 tails? Yes, you can well imagine this outcome happening also. After all, you are sitting there flipping this darn thing nearly 20,000 times. Your arm is getting tired. Your thumb is getting sore. You're bored. Once in a while, things will get thrown off. But notice that this outcome hardly ever happens. It happens, but rarely.

What would you think, however, if I gave you a coin, asked you to flip it 20 times, and, in that one instance or trial, you did come up with 17 heads and only 3 tails? Could it have happened by chance? Of course it could have. Another way of thinking about chance occurrences is to think of them as having unsystematic causes; that is, something caused them, but the causal process doesn't occur with any regularity. For example, maybe there was a solar flare, and the subatomic particles hitting the Earth at that instance caused the coin to land on heads 17 times. Or maybe you had too much

FIGURE 3.1 Frequency distribution of flipping a coin

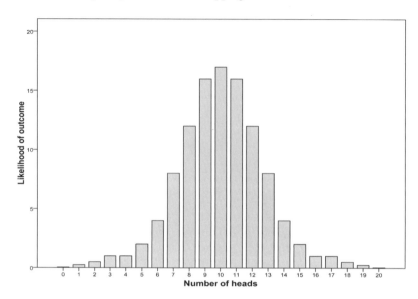

caffeine this morning, and you're a little shaky: poof! 17 heads. Or maybe a butterfly flapped its wings in China. You get the picture.

Let's return to the contingency table. You could program your computer (or . . . somebody could) to start with the chance distribution—that is, the 25 cases per cell—and then reallocate the cases to the cell over and over again randomly, 1,000 times. Actually, you could do this by hand yourself. Imagine for each of your 100 persons in the sample you flip a coin once to decide what his or her SES is going to be in this instance/trial and once to decide what his or her locus of control is going to be in this instance/trial. Then that's the cell into which you place that person. And you repeat this 1,000 times. Whether you do it or the computer does it, most of these instances or trials will tend toward a set of results that looks like the distribution of cases in parentheses in Table 3.2. And, once in a while, just like in the plain old coin-flipping exercise, the results you get will diverge dramatically from the even distribution of cases. But the results are still random. They just don't happen very often.

This process is the basic logic of statistical significance testing using the chi-square. You compare your observed distribution of cases to one that you

TABLE 3.3 Cross-tabulation of SES and locus of control, showing expected values based on the marginal distribution of each variable

			LOCUS OF CONTROL		TOTAL
			External	Internal	
SES	Low	Count	38	13	51
		Expected Count	29.1	21.9	51.0
	High	Count	19	30	49
		Expected Count	27.9	21.1	49.0
	Total	Count	57	43	100
		Expected Count	57.0	43.0	100.0

would anticipate *if* the allocation of cases in your table was random. The typical instance of calculating the chi-square is a little different from what is shown in Table 3.2 (although you can do it that way—see Leo Goodman's [1969] hierarchical model for analyzing a contingency table). You note that the marginals are not exactly 50-50 in the case of SES and that they diverge even more so from 50-50 in the case of locus of control. This situation means that the cases in the cells of the table on the basis of chance will not turn out to be 25; rather, they will be a function of what the associated marginal is.

I have redone this table as Table 3.3. To do this in SPSS, go back to "Crosstabs," under "Descriptive Statistics," under "Analyze." You should already have CatBairro in the rows slot and CatHLOC in the columns slot. Next, click the button marked "Cells" and in that menu, under "Counts," click a box for "Expected," along with "Observed." Click "Continue" to return to the "Crosstabs" menu. Next, click on the "Statistics" button. In the upper-left-hand corner you will see a box for "Chi-square." Click that box, click on continue to return to the main menu, and then click "OK."

In this table we have our original observed cases, and we have an estimate of the expected cases, taking into account the imperfect distribution of the marginals. These expected values are calculated by multiplying the respective marginals and dividing by the total; so for the upper-left-hand cell, you would multiply 57 x 51 and divide by 100, which equals 29.1. Then, the actual calculation for the chi-square statistic is

EQUATION 3.1

chi-square = SUM (observed – expected)^2 / expected.

Again, you calculate this difference between the observed and the expected for each cell and add them up to get your chi-square value. Keep in mind that what you are doing is very directly calculating the degree to which your observed distribution diverges from chance expectations. The value of chi-square for this example is given in Table 3.4. The table can be a little confusing, because, as I pointed out earlier, there are actually several different ways to calculate the chi-square on a given cross-tabulation. The good old, standard, garden-variety chi-square is the Pearson chi-square (so named for the early statistician Karl Pearson), which is shown in the first line of Table 3.4. Applying the formula given in Equation 3.1 gives you that value of 13.019. Don't worry about the column headed "df," or "degrees of freedom"—we'll deal with that later. The next column is the "asymptotic statistical significance," which, for our purposes, is just plain old statistical significance.

What do all these numbers mean? Here, we are again going to have to think about distributions. (This is part of the reason I introduced you to distributions and means and standard deviations right off the bat.) You need

TABLE 3.4 Values of chi-square for the cross-tabulation of SES and locus of control

	\multicolumn{5}{c}{CHI-SQUARE TESTS}
	Value	df	Asymp. Sig. (2-sided)	Exact Sig. (2-sided)	Exact Sig. (1-sided)
Pearson Chi-Square	13.019	1	.000		
Continuity Correction	11.602	1	.001		
Likelihood Ratio	13.324	1	.000		
Fisher's Exact Test				.001	.000
Linear-by-Linear Association	12.889	1	.000		
N of Valid Cases	100				

to learn to think in terms of everything having a distribution. The normal distribution is just one kind of distribution, one that works as a pretty good model for the way many observations in the world are distributed. Other things have different kinds of distributions, and the chi-square distribution has its own. Remember how we imagined generating a distribution of differences for the (observed − expected)? Well, mathematical statisticians have calculated the theoretical distribution of chi-square, assuming no association between the two variables (that is, as if every cell had exactly what you would expect by chance, taking into account how the variables are distributed).

Figure 3.2 shows what the chi-square distribution looks like. This is a kind of "thought experiment." Imagine that, in Ribeirão Preto, in the whole community, there really is no relationship between SES and locus of control. Then what we do is repeat the random samples of 100 persons 1,000 times. The distribution shown in Figure 3.2 is the distribution of chi-square values themselves *if and only if* there was really no association between SES and locus of control in the city. This distribution is logically equivalent to generating a distribution of coin flips with an honest coin. In Figure 3.2 an area of the curve formed by the distribution of chi-square values is shaded. This shaded area is for a value of chi-square equal to or larger than 3.84. Just eye-balling Figure 3.2, we see that this value, or one larger than it, would not occur that often. Think about this as analogous to the univariate distribution of flipping a coin. Being out on the tail of the distribution of chi-square is similar to getting 17 heads and 3 tails. It happens, but not very often.

With our imagined contingency table where there is no relationship, in 1,000 different replications you will get values of chi-square equal to 3.84 just by chance, but not very often. In fact, the value of chi-square equal to 3.84 would occur only about 5 times in 100 different replications. The actual

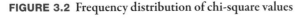

FIGURE 3.2 Frequency distribution of chi-square values

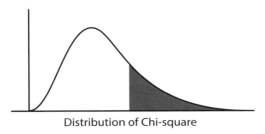

Distribution of Chi-square

value of chi-square that we obtained—13.019—would be obtained under these circumstances only 1 time in 1,000 replications *by chance, if there really was no relationship between SES and HLOC in the whole population of the city.*

Well, we didn't do this study 1,000 times, did we? We did it once. Could we have gotten these results purely by chance? Of course! We could be so unlucky, so benighted, so frowned on by the gods of probability that the universe has played a nasty trick on us and given us a set of data, making it appear as if there is a relationship between SES and locus of control. Yes, this could have happened. But, was it *likely* to have happened? No. Given that we did our study just this one time, and the distribution of all chi-squares for doing this study indicates that you get a value that large only 1 time in 1,000 when there's really no relationship, suggests that, indeed, the more logical inference is that there really is a relationship between SES and locus of control. The universe just got a little less chaotic.

In fact, if you do a little arithmetic, it turns out that, if you live in a higher SES neighborhood, you are almost 5 times more likely to report an internal locus of control than if you live in a lower SES neighborhood.

Before concluding, I will go back and add a little explanation of the mysterious **df**, or **degrees of freedom.** This concept can be more easily understood in relation to contingency table analysis, because it becomes more transparent there. Looking back at Table 3.3, we again see that there are 51 people in the low SES neighborhoods and 49 people in the high SES neighborhoods. By the same token, there are 57 people with an external locus of control and 43 people with an internal locus of control. In contingency table analysis, these marginal distributions are regarded as "fixed"; that is, that's just the way it is. There are those proportions of people in Ribeirão Preto, period. What can vary, however, is how SES and HLOC go together. Just because you know how each variable varies, you don't know how the variables will co-vary (remember that word, because the notion of co-variation, or **covariance**, will come in handy later). Now, think about the fact that we know that 38 people fall into the low SES/external locus of control category. Knowing that, you can look at the table and see that you now also know what the other observed values will be in that table. The number 38 has to be added to something else to sum to 57 at the bottom. Similarly, it has to be added to something else to sum to 51 in the right-hand marginals, because these numbers are fixed. So, once you know the contents of one cell—that is, that there are 38 low SES/

external people—every other number in the table can be easily calculated. There is, in other words, only 1 degree of freedom in the table.

The theoretical distribution of chi-square changes slightly depending on the number of degrees of freedom in the table. We will encounter the concept of degrees of freedom again, in contexts in which its meaning is not quite so intuitive. But whenever you run across it, it is telling you the same thing: the limits within which your data can vary.

SUMMARY

The aim of this chapter has been to introduce you to thinking bivariately, to the chi-square, and especially to the meaning of statistical significance. The essence of statistical significance testing is the comparison of your observed data to a model for what your data would look like if chaos ruled the universe (or, at least, if there was no systematic relationship between the two variables you are looking at). The beauty of exploring this meaning in the example of contingency tables and the chi-square is that you can just look at it. You get to see the model of chance right before your eyes.

Another way to think about the logic of statistical significance testing is in terms of your confidence in what you are saying about the world. You want to argue that experience in the world is associated with the development of the psychological orientation called *locus of control*. You may do a series of open-ended interviews with members of a lower-class neighborhood in Ribeirão Preto in which you ask about success in school or work, and your respondents express a sense of resignation about not being able to continue their educations or not being able to get the kind of job they want. They conclude, quite sensibly, that their own efforts are at least diminished, if not totally frustrated, by the world around them. Then, however, you interview several persons from upper-middle class neighborhoods who describe their success in school, passing the *vestibular* (the notoriously difficult university entrance exam in Brazil), and going on to success in their chosen profession. They conclude that their own effort, perseverance, and talent have led to their success. You infer that the opportunities afforded, or not, by socioeconomic background have contributed to (although not completely determined) class differences in a psychological sense of self-efficacy that is termed *locus of control*.

The problem is: how confident are you in your assertions based on your case studies? Are the findings that you have generated reliable, in the sense that with more interviews your observations could be repeated? Selecting a representative sample, measuring the variables systematically, and analyzing the data statistically allow you to answer that question. Yes, the association of SES and locus of control is **statistically reliable** in that you would be unlikely to encounter such an association by chance. And, as Mlodinow (2009) argues, this is not a trivial demonstration.

This recognition is a pretty good addition of confidence to your assertion. Also, remember that we are still engaged in our original enterprise of trying to guess João's locus of control. By adding another variable, which is more information about him, we can reduce the uncertainty in our guess. This addition of information increases our confidence in what we can say about the world.

The intuitive appeal of the chi-square can be a bit seductive. Some people, once they've learned it, want to use nothing else. This inclination can mean that they go around chopping up their data into various sorts of dichotomies, which can be a bit dicey. Take, for example, the variable HLOC. We, of course, know that it has a nice spread of values, but what if it didn't? What if it had a tall, skinny distribution with all the values bunched up around the values of 7 or 8. In this situation, thinking of persons as being on either side of a dichotomy, of being "high" versus "low," or "external" versus "internal," becomes a bit arbitrary, to say the least. If you were to calculate an average HLOC for low SES folks, and an average HLOC for high SES folks, those values might turn out not to be all that different. If that were the case, by forcing them to be on one side of a dichotomy or the other, you can inadvertently introduce a pattern into the data that is not really there. So, you need to have a pretty good justification for transforming a continuous variable such as HLOC into a dichotomy. Sometimes a valid justification lies in the distribution of the data. If the distribution of your data diverges dramatically from a normal distribution, you may need to fall back a level of measurement. Another valid justification for dichotomizing your data will lie in your theory. You may hypothesize that people have to achieve a certain threshold level on a variable before other kinds of effects kick in. For example, in the case of SES, you might hypothesize that a part of the influence on locus of control is the higher education that higher SES affords. Perhaps the two less well-off neighborhoods in Ribeirão Preto don't really differ from each other with respect to level of education, and the two more well-off neighborhoods don't differ from each other. The real differences that exist are between the two sets of neighborhoods. Therefore, the true causal potential, with respect to influencing locus of control, lies in that low SES– high SES contrast alone. Then you would be justified in dichotomizing that variable.

Such insight may come to you from your ethnographic work or from your theoretical work. Whatever the source of inspiration, you need to think carefully about what you are doing in all phases of data analysis, including such seemingly innocuous decisions as whether or not to dichotomize a variable.

The Logic of Statistical Significance Testing: Analysis of Variance

In the last chapter we examined how, using contingency table analysis and the chi-square statistic, we could compare our observed results against a model of chance. To do so, we had to step down a level of measurement, converting the continuous measure of locus of control to a simple dichotomy: external versus internal. And these are merely heuristic labels to boot. We don't really know what it is to be, in some essential sense, "internal" or "external." Rather, what we are doing is ordering people along a continuum from a tendency to respond to questions in an "external way" to responding in an "internal way." It would be good to analyze the data in such a way that we can both have some information about our respondents that improves our guessing about their locus of control and retain the conceptualization of locus of control as a continuum—a more-or-less sort of psychological state—rather than slipping into an often bad habit of thinking about it as some kind of Platonic essence. Furthermore, treating locus of control as a continuum would enhance our ability to detect any association, because we have more information. The analysis of variance enables us to examine the association of a categorical variable and a continuous variable.

Let's look at the histogram of locus of control again, shown in Figure 4.1. Another way of thinking about that distribution is: why in the world is everyone so different? For sure, even if people were more homogeneous in their locus of control orientations, there would be some variability just by chance, but in that case you would expect people to be more closely packed around the mean. But they aren't. If we assume that we have a pretty good sampling of statements that capture the concept of locus of control,

FIGURE 4.1 Histogram of locus of control scores

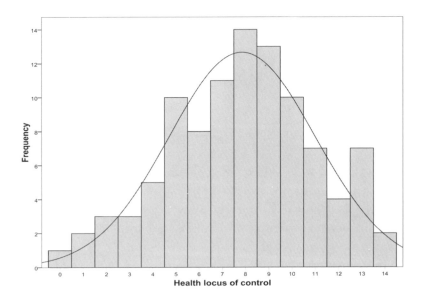

people are spread across the entire spectrum of possible ways of expressing this psychological orientation. They cover the theoretical spread. Why in the world isn't everyone just closer to being average?

This is another way of thinking about statistical analysis, which is the search for those factors that lead to differentiation among people. One way to think about this in relation to Figure 4.1 is to imagine that we are not really looking at a single distribution. Rather, hiding in that distribution are some subdistributions, and a person's membership in some group that is described by a subdistribution is the reason that he or she is so far from the mean. In Figure 4.2 I have superimposed some subdistributions to represent this idea.

What might these subdistributions be? As I mentioned at the outset, socioeconomic status can be conceptualized in a variety of ways in Brazil. Neighborhood of residence is one, which we used in the last chapter. Educational level completed is another, and in this chapter we will use it, broken into three categories. It would be easy to imagine that these three subdistributions correspond to a standard way that Brazilians talk about years of completed education: primary school education, secondary school education, and an advanced education (any kind of schooling beyond

FIGURE 4.2 Histogram of locus of control scores with hypothetical
subdistributions superimposed

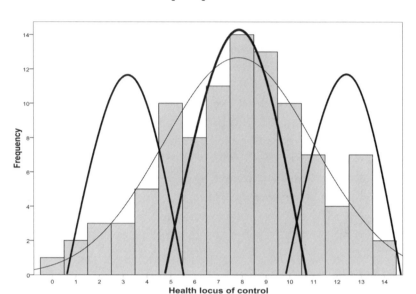

secondary but especially a university education). In the small subset of data from 1991 that we are working with here, 60% of the people have a primary school education; 15% of the sample a secondary school education; and 25% of the sample an advanced education (in our most recent Brazil data from 2011, that breaks down as about a third of the sample in each group, but remember that we are oversampling upper-income neighborhoods, which is actually going to skew the data a bit toward the more highly educated).

The sociologist Hubert Blalock (1960) presented an interesting way to think about this analysis. He started with the same question I did: why isn't everyone the same? I've placed an *x* on one tail of the lowest subdistribution in Figure 4.3 to indicate a single respondent (let's say João again). Why is João so far away from the overall mean for the distribution, as I have indicated in Figure 4.3? In arithmetic, we can express this as

EQUATION 4.1

$$X_1 - M.$$

Symbolically, this little phrase simply asks the question: why is João different from the mean?

Looking at Figure 4.4, we can see that there is a reasonable explanation for why he is so different from the overall mean: it's because he belongs to that particular subdistribution, and that subdistribution has its own mean, which is different from the overall mean. In Figure 4.4, I have indicated the subdistribution mean as "M_1," and I have relabeled the overall mean for the distribution as "M_G," because in treatments of statistics it is often referred to as "the grand mean." So, in other words, what we are guessing here is that there is something about having the characteristics that people in that subdistribution share that leads them to have values of HLOC that are more similar to one another than to the rest of the distribution, and hence they have their own subgroup mean. We can express this in arithmetic:

EQUATION 4.2

$$X_1 - M_G = M_1 - M_G.$$

FIGURE 4.3 Histogram of locus of control scores, comparing one respondent and the mean for the distribution

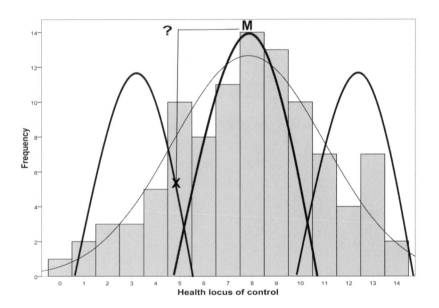

FIGURE 4.4 Histogram of locus of control scores, comparing one subgroup mean and the mean for the distribution

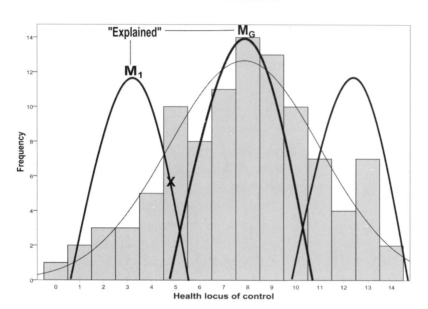

So, in other words, João is different from the grand mean because he belongs to a subgroup that has a mean that is different from the grand mean—that is, a subgroup with a primary school education. We have **explained** this difference between João's HLOC score and the overall or grand mean because he has a primary school education.

Of course, we have not explained this difference entirely. Why? Because we still haven't taken into account that João has an HLOC score that is different from that of his own subgroup. In Figure 4.5 I have labeled this particular difference the **unexplained** difference, because we literally have no idea why it is that João is different from his own subgroup. In arithmetic, we can add this notion to our little equation:

EQUATION 4.3

$$X_1 - M_G = (M_1 - M_G) + (X_1 - M_1).$$

FIGURE 4.5 Histogram of locus of control scores, comparing one subgroup mean and the mean for the distribution, and one respondent and the mean for one subgroup

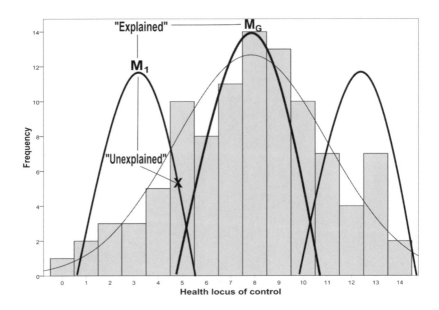

There are two things to keep in mind here. The first is that this little bit of arithmetic is illustrative. In fact, what we are doing is calculating different sets of the sums of deviations for all our sampled respondents. Recall that summing these squared deviations enables us to get at the variation in the sample—which leads us to the second thing to keep in mind: in essence, what we are doing here is decomposing the variation present in the sample into several components. On the left-hand side of the equals sign we have a term representing the total variation in the sample. On the right-hand side of the equation we have two terms, the first representing the variation associated with being in a particular group versus other groups, and the second representing the variation that is left over inside that group.

The little bit of arithmetic, first proposed by Blalock, is a handy way to get a conceptual handle on what's going on here. And, of course, it's not the way that things are actually done. (I say "of course" because nothing is ever as straightforward as it seems.) Rather than decomposing the over-all variation into a component accounting for the difference between the group mean and the overall mean, what we actually do is calculate the variation per se. Think about it this way: there is a total amount of variation in the data represented by the different scores that people have on HLOC. This is a sum that just stands for all of the variation. Then you think about that variation as coming from two sources. One of those sources is the variation within the subgroups that, frankly, we don't really understand (yet). The second is the variation between the groups, treated as groups that we do understand (or, at least, we think we do). The **between-groups variation** and the **within-groups variation** will always add up to the **total variation.**

Once we have come up with these estimates of the different contributions to the variation, we can do something else with them, which is to calculate a ratio. What would you expect the ratio of the explained variation to the unexplained variation to be if being a member of any particular group had no relationship whatsoever with locus of control? In essence, identifying a group mean would then not help at all in accounting for why somebody is different from the overall mean, because he is as likely to be very different from his own group mean as he is from the overall sample mean. In this case, the variation labeled "Explained" in Figure 4.5 and the variation labeled "Unexplained" are likely to be pretty much the same, and hence the ratio is going to be around 1.0.

But, if the differences between the group mean and the overall sample mean are large—and, more accurately, the variation between the group means is large—relative to the variation within the groups, then that ratio is likely to be larger than 1.0. Look at Figure 4.5 and imagine the subgroup means getting farther and farther apart, and imagine the subgroup distributions getting skinnier and skinnier. As this happens, the ratio of explained-to-unexplained gets larger and larger.

Think back now to the "observed-minus-the-expected" difference in the chi-square. The unexplained or within-groups variation here is sort of like the expected values in the chi-square, in the sense that if belonging to a subgroup did not make any difference in where a person is in the overall distribution, you would anticipate that the within-groups variation would be just as large as the between-groups variation. A large within-groups variation is, in essence, your model of chance. But then, if you find that the within-groups variation is substantially smaller than the between-groups variation, you have beaten chance, because group membership accounts for a big chunk of that variation. This is the essence of the analysis of variance.

As in the case of the chi-square, the ratio of the explained-to-the-unexplained variation—which is called the **F-ratio,** in honor of Sir Ronald Fisher—has its own distribution. You can imagine repeating the survey in Ribeirão Preto 1,000 times, and, if it really made no difference for anyone's locus of control to be in a particular subgroup, you would be unlikely, by chance, to find a very large ratio of explained-to-unexplained variation. But if you do that study once and you find a large ratio, although it still may have occurred simply by chance, you can have a certain confidence that it is unlikely to have done so.

There are actually several ways to do analysis of variance (abbreviated **ANOVA**) in SPSS. The simplest way is go to "Analyze" and then "Compare Means" and then within that menu to "Means." In the drop-down menu place HLOC in the Dependent List box and EDU (for education) in the Independent List box. Under Options check "Anova table and eta" (eta is a correlation coefficient that can be used with ANOVA, but don't worry about that until the end of the next chapter). Return to the "Means" menu and click "OK" to produce the output shown in Table 4.1.

In the upper panel of Table 4.1 the subgroup means for people with primary, secondary, and advanced education are given, along with the overall sample mean and the respective standard deviations. As we can see, people with a primary education have considerably lower HLOC scores relative to the overall sample mean and relative to the other groups. People with a secondary or with an advanced level of education have HLOC scores that are higher than the overall sample mean and higher than persons with a primary education. In the lower panel of Table 4.1 the calculation of the F-ratio is given. What we have been talking about as explained and unexplained variation corresponds to what in this table is labeled "Mean Square." It turns out, if you do the arithmetic, you can get away with not doing all the subtracting of means, either at the sample level or at the group level, in order to get the estimates of variation that you need. All you have to do is square the values that people have and add them up. But you do that in two different ways. You do it within the groups, literally by squaring everybody's values and adding them up, and you do it between groups, taking the group-level sums, squaring those, and adding them up. This approach gives you the two estimates of variation, between and within. But remember the notion of degrees of freedom. The within-groups variation has a lot more ways it can vary, given that it is estimated from all the individuals. So, it has a larger

TABLE 4.1 Analysis of variance of locus of control by education

REPORT			
HEALTH LOCUS OF CONTROL			
Education	Mean	N	Std. Deviation
primary	6.7000	60	3.15852
secondary	9.0667	15	1.710992
advanced	9.8800	25	2.48864
Total	7.8500	100	3.15068

ANOVA TABLE						
		Sum of Squares	df	Mean Square	F	Sig.
Health locus of control * Education	Between Groups	204.577	2	102.288	12.750	0.000
	Within Groups	778.173	97	8.022		
	Total	982.750	99			

number of degrees of freedom. The between-groups variation, based as it is on summed and squared values, has, in our example, only a couple of ways of varying (because if you add up two of the group estimates of variation, you have to know the third, because you already know the total variation in the sample). In Table 4.1, the between-groups estimate of the variation gets divided by 2, because that's the group-level number of degrees of freedom. The within-groups estimate of the variation gets divided by 97, because of the much larger number of contributors to that calculation.

So, these estimates of contributions to variation (the *sums of squares*) are divided by their respective degrees of freedom to get the "Mean Square" values in Table 4.1, which are the estimates of between-group variation and within-group variation. If you divide 102.288 by 8.022, you'll get 12.75; this is the value of the F-ratio. There is a specific, theoretically derived distribution of F for the number of degrees of freedom that you have. This value of F is way out on the tail of all the possible values of F you might find in these data *if* there really was no relationship between education and locus of control. Your conclusion? Well, you might have gotten these results solely by chance, because you are actually the most unlucky researcher in the whole world. But you would be that unlucky only less than 1 time in 1,000 replications of the study. So, you give yourself a break and conclude that there might be something about education that influences locus of control.

There is a nice way to visualize this analysis. In SPSS, go to the Menu Bar and click on "Graphs." Go to the "Legacy Dialogues" and then to "Error Bar." Within the "Error Bar" menu click on the box labeled "Simple" and click the "Define" button at the bottom of the menu. In the new menu provided, put HLOC in the "Variable" box, put EDU in the "Category axis" box, and then click OK. The result is shown in Figure 4.6. The horizontal axis groups the sample respondents into the three groups based on education. The vertical axis is graded from external locus of control at the bottom to internal locus of control at the top (or, the number of questions to which a respondent gives an internal locus of control answer). Within the graph, for each group defined by educational attainment, the mean value of locus of control from Table 4.1 is indicated.

FIGURE 4.6 Error bar graph of locus of control by level of completed education

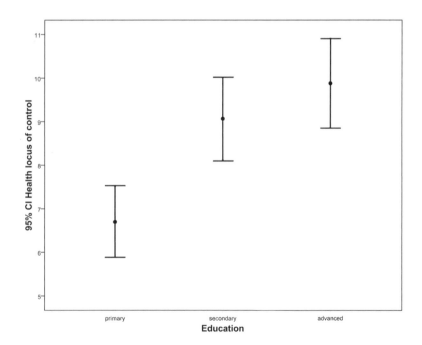

Around the mean (marked by a small open circle) are bars that indicate the 95% confidence intervals. You already know what these are (Chapter 3). The width of the bars is defined by the **standard error of the mean** within each education subgroup. The standard error of the mean is just the same as the standard deviation *except* that it applies to a whole distribution of potential means or averages. Imagine that you have sampled these 100 Ribeirão Pretanhos 1,000 times, and each time you have calculated the mean within each education group. You would then have 1,000 mean values within each group. You could take the average of these averages and get a standard deviation for the average of the averages: this is the standard error. The 95% confidence intervals around the subgroup means in Figure 4.6 are, roughly, what a bracket of +2 standard errors and −2 standard errors around the mean would look like (actually, for calculating the interval in which, 95% of the time in repeated samples, you would find the mean for that group you take ±1.96 standard errors—but 2 is easier to remember). Another way to think about Figure 4.6 is as three different univariate distributions, but lying on their sides. The histogram describing the within-groups distributions would also be sideways, and the tails of the distributions would be marked by the error bars.

So what? Remember trying to guess João's level of internal locus of control? Knowing nothing but the average of the sample as a whole, that's all you can guess. And you know you are going to be off by a pretty wide margin. But now, when I challenge you to guess his locus of control, you ask me: "Well, what's his educational level?" I respond that he has a primary school level of education. You reply that you think his locus of control score would be 6.7 or, more reasonably, around 7, and that you are pretty sure that it is somewhere between 6 and 8. In fact, you say, 95% of the time someone with a primary school education is going to come back with a mean level of locus of control between 6 and 8. Remember that, when you knew only the univariate distribution you would have guessed a score of 8, and you would have been confident that 95% of the time the score would be between 1 and 14. You have, in other words, reduced the error and uncertainty in your estimation. It is still an estimate, to be sure, but it's a much better one. You have graduated from guessing that someone is going to win the Super Bowl to guessing who is going to win and by what margin.

There is something else interesting you can see in Figure 4.6. When you get a significant result, as we did in ANOVA, you know for sure that at least one of the groups is statistically significantly different from at least one of the other groups. Any guesses as to which one? If you answered the primary education group, you were absolutely right. Why? Well, as you can see, the confidence intervals around the primary education group do not overlap with either of the other education groups. That is, even in a sample in which the mean for the primary education group was as high as it reasonably could be expected to be, and even in a sample in which the mean for the secondary education group was as low as it reasonably could be expected to be, they (the error bars) would not overlap. This lack of overlap in distributions is the essence of statistical significance, represented graphically. The level of statistical significance, well less than 1 chance in 1,000 replications, is a result of this lack of overlap between the range of variation for the means within the groups. In some data the differences will not be quite so extreme, but you will still have reasonable levels of statistical significance, such as the famous p < .05, which means that you would encounter these results fewer than 5 times in 100 replications by chance (more about levels of statistical significance later on). My point is that you could eyeball Figure 4.6 and know that the differences are statistically significant.

My aim in this chapter has been to introduce you to the analysis of variance but, even more important, to introduce you to the idea of decomposing variability in a sample into different components and using that, in this case, to evaluate statistical significance. This general idea that there are different components that make up the overall variability in a sample will prove to be very important.

If you have read anything at all in statistics, you may be wondering why I haven't been talking about **Student's *t*-test.** In most introductory treatments of statistics the *t*-test is almost always introduced first, followed by the analysis of variance. It is only later on that you learn that the *t*-test is actually a special case of the analysis of variance, one in which there are only two groups. In that special instance, there is a specific formula that can be used that is not nearly as complex and daunting as the set of computations needed to do an analysis of variance by hand. Since we are not interested in computations but rather in a conceptual understanding, it makes more sense to go straight to **ANOVA**, since it is the more general model. It turns out that t is actually the square root of F, if both were to be calculated on the same set of data comparing two groups on a continuous variable.

Just to make that case clear, let's look at two groups and HLOC. In this example I return to the SES dichotomy, based on neighborhood of residence, that we used in Chapter 3. The error bar graph for the difference between the two neighborhood groups in mean health locus of control is shown in Figure 4.7. That difference, given that the confidence intervals don't overlap at all, clearly indicates statistical significance. If we calculate that statistical significance using ANOVA, we get $F = 20.629$; $df = 1, 98$; $p < .0001$. If we calculate that statistical significance using a t-test, we get $t = 4.542$, $df = 98$, $p < .0001$. And, if you square 4.542 you get 20.629. Again, the t-test is just a special case of ANOVA when there are two groups.

What we have done here is called **one-way analysis of variance**, because we are just comparing a set of groups defined by a single variable, in this case education. Frequently in ANOVA there is what is called a **post-hoc**, or "after-the-fact," test. Reconsider Figure 4.6: you can see that people with a primary education have a level of HLOC lower than either the secondary or advanced education groups but that the secondary and advanced education groups don't look so different from each other. You can see that because of the way the confidence intervals overlap. Thus, the truly significant differences here are between primary and secondary, and primary and advanced, but not between secondary and advanced. What a post-hoc test does is the same as what you have done with your own eyes, only statistically. You can think of the F-ratio as telling you "yup, there's something going on here," while the post-hoc test tells you precisely where the differences are. Why, you may ask yourself, don't you just run a bunch of specific comparisons right off the bat? You could use the t-test to compare specific groups, and all you would have to do is three t-tests to nail it down, right?

As you may be gleaning by now, statistics is all about living in fear of "capitalizing on chance." That's why you go through the whole rigmarole of statistical significance testing, to determine if some difference you think is important is actually likely to be statistically reliable, based on the assumption that if it isn't statistically reliable it's unlikely to be theoretically important. If you are trying to unpack a causal process—such as how experience in the social environment alters one's psychological state regarding a sense of control—you really don't want to be looking at unique, freaky, happenstance occurrences. You want stuff that is statistically reliable.

This thinking gets extended to running statistical tests. The idea is that the more tests you run, the more likely it is you will stumble across something

FIGURE 4.7 Error bar graph of locus of control by SES

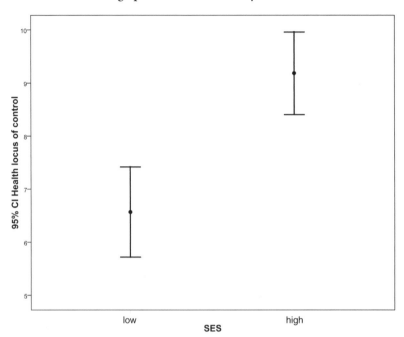

by chance. Granted, running three pair-wise *t*-tests isn't really running a lot of tests, but that's how the thinking goes. So, you run the overall ANOVA— sometimes called the **protected F-test**—and then you run the post-hoc tests.

The world of ANOVA can get a whole lot more complicated really fast. Consider **factorial analysis of variance,** which is what you do when you want to look at more than one independent variable at the same time. Imagine that we did a cross-tabulation of education with something like gender; then in the cells of the cross-tabulation you would have the mean of locus of control for that subset of people. In this way you could look at the combined effects of having a particular level of education and of being male or female on locus of control. Actually, that's a very interesting and important thing to do, in the sense that the world is sufficiently complicated that it is unlikely that any one variable is going to explain the sorts of things that we are interested in. But that situation is too far afield for us; just think about decomposing variability into its components. That's enough for now.

SUMMARY

In this chapter we approached the task of guessing João's level of internal locus of control from a different angle: by suggesting that he belongs to a group, unified by their experience in the world as conditioned by their educational level, and that this group has a tendency to develop a particular outlook on the world. We could evaluate this guess—or this **hypothesis**—by comparing how much education groups, as groups, tend to differ, relative to how much individuals tend to differ from each other within those groups. When there is variation between the groups that exceeds the variation among the individuals within the groups, our expectation is confirmed— that indeed being in a particular group defined by education conditions one's psychological outlook.

A final note on language: I've heard some people get vexed by the use of such terms as "explained" variance in ANOVA and other statistical techniques. They argue that this use of the word is misleading and that it lulls students into a false sense of security in what they are doing. It is true that to "explain" something is a complicated issue in the philosophy of the social sciences. Just what constitutes an adequate explanation for a particular phenomenon is no small conundrum. It should be clear, however, that the statistical sense of explaining variation is simply a matter of knowing where to allocate that variation. In ANOVA we are saying that we know that we can allocate some of the overall variation in locus of control to the educational groups, as groups. Yet we still don't know where to allocate all the variation that remains within the groups. In that sense, the variation between the groups is explained, and the variation within the groups is unexplained. Nobody should be confused that using the term *explained* in the statistical sense signifies a deeper theoretical explanation of why people with different education levels have different psychological orientations.

The Logic of the Correlation Coefficient

Thus far we have considered what in statistics are traditionally regarded as **tests of difference.** That is, we have groups defined by socioeconomic status or education, and we are interested in any differences between them in locus of control, treated as a continuous variable in the case of **ANOVA** and treated as a dichotomy in the case of the chi-square. What do we do in the case of two continuous variables? Here we turn to what is referred to as a **test of association** in statistics—more specifically, the *Pearson correlation coefficient.* With the correlation coefficient we will be able to determine if there is any systematic association between two continuous variables, the strength or degree of association, and the direction of the association.

To begin, we need another continuous variable that can be thought of as an independent variable. We will use *cultural consonance in lifestyle* (Dressler, Balieiro, & Dos Santos 1998). Cultural consonance is the degree to which individuals in their own beliefs and behaviors approximate the prototypes for belief and behavior that are encoded in shared cultural models (Dressler 2007). Briefly stated: the rationale behind this measure is based in a cognitive culture theory. Individuals in any society share cognitive structures we call *cultural models*: skeletal, schematic, stripped-down representations of some cultural domain, including the elements within that domain and the relationships among those elements. We have found in several studies in Brazil that people have well-developed ideas about a good lifestyle (*estilo da vida* in Portuguese). A *lifestyle,* in the sense originally used by Thorstein Veblen (1912) and more recently by Pierre Bourdieu (1984), consists of the material goods people accumulate and the leisure time activities in which they participate in order to have what is collectively regarded as a "good life." Achieving a certain lifestyle is one of those life-span developmental goals associated with advanced capitalist market societies. A lifestyle is a public, observable indication of how well we are doing/have done in our lives with respect to achieving what Veblen called a "decent" (note the moral connotation) level of economic well-being.

To determine if there was a shared cultural model of lifestyle, we first interviewed people about their goals and aspirations in this domain, and from these interviews we generated a representative list of items (including owning a house, a car, a computer, and other items, as well as leisure activities such as going to the movies, belonging to a sports club, being able to go out to eat on occasion, and other similar activities). We then had people rate the importance of these items for having a good life. Cultural consensus analysis was used to test for a shared cultural model of a good lifestyle. (I discuss cultural consensus analysis in Chapter 7.) This analysis confirmed that people shared a basic model of what one needs to live a comfortable life (see Dressler, Dos Santos, & Balieiro [1996] for a more detailed discussion).

Then, to measure cultural consonance in the survey that we have been using in this book, we asked people if they actually owned the material goods rated as important for a good life and if they engaged in the leisure time activities that were rated as important (remember that what is regarded as "important" was generated within Ribeirão Preto). Simply counting up the number of items that people report tells you how close these people are to fulfilling the shared cultural model in their own behavior. To simplify the measure, I have taken all the items (18 out of 39) that were rated at least "somewhat important" in the cultural consensus analysis and just counted the number of those that each respondent reported. I then divided by 18 and multiplied by 100 to give a measure that varies between 0 and 100. The larger the number, the closer an individual is to the shared cultural model of lifestyle in his or her own behavior. Figure 5.1 shows a histogram of cultural consonance in lifestyle. Again, it's not a perfect normal distribution, but it's not bad for the real world.

I am guessing here that the greater an individual's cultural consonance, the more in control of his or her own life s/he will feel. How can we evaluate this? The first thing we can do is create a **scatterplot.** To do this in SPSS, go to "Graphs," select "Legacy Dialogs," and select "Scatter/Dot." From the menu shown select "Simple Scatter." Click on "Define," and you will see a new menu. Put HLOC in the box for the y-axis, and put CCLS in the box for the x-axis, and click OK.

FIGURE 5.1 Histogram of cultural consonance in lifestyle scores

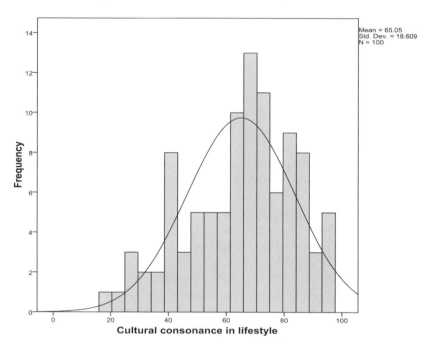

The result will be a figure like Figure 5.2. What we have done is to plot each individual in the sample simultaneously by their values on locus of control and their values on cultural consonance. Remember that each individual in the sample has two values, one for each variable, and we are simply locating each person in space simultaneously by each value. Looking at Figure 5.2, we see what appears to be a general trend, such that persons who have lower values on cultural consonance tend to have lower values on locus of control, and persons who have higher values on cultural consonance tend to have higher values on locus of control. Obviously there is not a one-to-one correspondence here. But the trend seems to exist.

How can we more precisely identify this trend? One way would be to draw a line in the graph to visually represent this trend. Looking at Figure 5.2 we quickly see a number of places we could probably put that line—but there is a more systematic way to do it. In fact, only a single line can be drawn in Figure 5.2 that satisfies the useful condition of coming closer to all the points in the graph than any other line. Using calculus (which, fortunately,

FIGURE 5.2 Scatterplot of health locus of control scores and cultural consonance in lifestyle scores

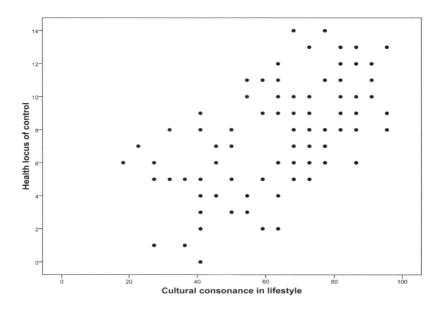

we neither have to do ourselves nor necessarily understand all that well), we can fit a line to those points that minimizes the sum of the squared deviations of the points around that line. By now, you should be at least used to, if not comfortable with, the idea of calculating deviations from some point and squaring those deviations to get rid of negative numbers. Well, here we go again! SPSS, or whatever computer program you use, will calculate and position a line such that the sum of the squared deviations of individual data points, for each of the 100 individuals in the sample, from a corresponding point on that line will be at a minimum.

Figure 5.3 shows that line. At this point, I'm going to ask you to think back to your high school algebra class (probably the one you took as a freshman in high school). In it, you learned that a straight line could be represented by an equation of the following type:

EQUATION 5.1

$Y = a + bx.$

FIGURE 5.3 Scatterplot of locus of control scores and cultural consonance in lifestyle scores, including the linear regression line

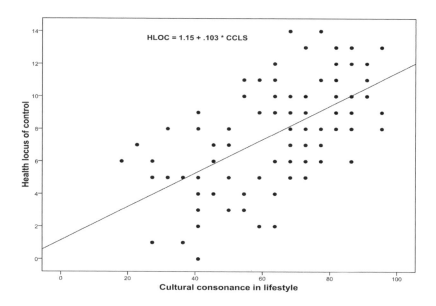

I've set this equation apart because we are going to come back to it over and over again. This equation—and again, it's nothing particularly fancy; it's what high school freshmen have to learn—says that we can calculate the value of the variable representing the *y*-axis, or vertical axis, by knowing where the line crosses that axis (*a* in the equation) and by knowing how much we have to multiply values of the variable representing the *x*-axis, or horizontal axis, by (*b* in the equation, or the "slope" of the line). In our particular example this is

---

EQUATION 5.2

$$HLOC = 1.15 + .105CC,$$

or, to calculate values of locus of control, we multiply a person's value on cultural consonance by .105 and add 1.15. Welcome to the basic statistical model for representing the world around us! (I could not resist throwing that in right here; it's something I'm going to come back to in some detail later on.)

I emphasize here again what we have done. We've gone out and collected a bunch of data on locus of control and cultural consonance. We seem to think that cultural consonance might have something to do with a person's locus of control, so we have plotted individuals in a graph simultaneously by their values on each variable. Eyeballing the graph, we feel vindicated, because there does seem to be a trend there. Next, with the courteous help of SPSS, we plotted a line in there that has the happy characteristic of coming closer to all the points than any other possible line. Remember that there is one and only one line that satisfies that criterion. After doing all that, we figured out what the equation for that line is. Keep in mind, however, that *the equation describes the line, not the data.* The line is a model to represent the data; it is not the data.

I take pains to describe it this way because we can have the unfortunate tendency to fall into the trap of thinking that we have discovered something about nature here. In a sense, we have; we have discovered that there appears to be a systematic tendency for locus of control to become more internal as a person's cultural consonance increases. But—and this is a big "but"—we are fitting those data to a statistical model that employs the equation for a straight line. In other words, we are using what we know about straight lines to think about what we don't know—how cultural consonance is associated with locus of control.

I hope you are thinking about an obvious question now—that is, is that straight line any good? Remember that the mathematics here does not care one bit about whether this model is a good, bad, or half-way decent representation of the data. The mathematics, as implemented by SPSS, will work. If the data in Figure 5.3 were a completely random scatter of points, SPSS would still fit a straight line to them. There will always be a line that fits the criterion of minimizing the sum of the squared deviations about it— which is called, by the way, a **least-squares fit**. But whether that representation of the data is good, bad, or indifferent is a matter of no concern whatsoever to the mathematics or the computer program. It is of concern only to you.

So, how do we figure out if that fit is any good? We are trying to determine if knowing cultural consonance is of any utility in guessing somebody's locus of control. Think back to Chapter 1: if all we knew about was the distribution of locus of control, then our best guess for somebody's locus of control would be the mean or average locus of control. So, let's put this best guess into the figure (see Figure 5.4). Think of it as the baseline from which we start guessing—and remember, we know we are likely to be wrong when just guessing the mean. Hence, we can already start to think about the differences between actually observed data points and the mean for the distribution. We will think about this difference as the **total variation** (as indicated in Figure 5.5).

I've pointed to two data points in Figure 5.5, one with low locus of control and one with high locus of control. Both of these data points— people, remember—are quite different from the mean (I also indicate the mean as it corresponds to each data point), and our question always is why. Why are people so different? Right now, we are guessing they are so different because they are also so different in their cultural consonance. We have points in Figures 5.3–5.5 that indicate what a person's locus of control *would be* if her value on that variable were a simple function of cultural consonance. If a person's locus of control were a simple function

---

FIGURE 5.4 Scatterplot of locus of control scores and cultural consonance in lifestyle scores, including the linear regression line and a line indicating the mean of locus of control scores

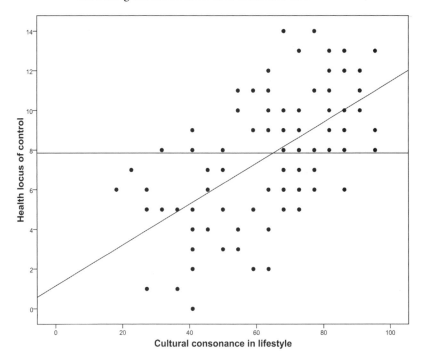

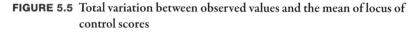

FIGURE 5.5 Total variation between observed values and the mean of locus of control scores

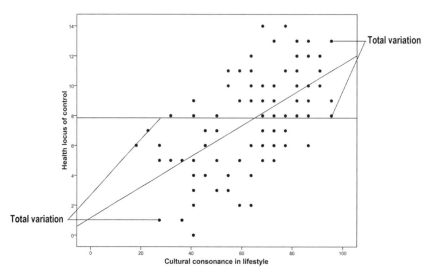

of her cultural consonance, her score would fall exactly on the straight line (assuming that the relationship between cultural consonance and locus of control can be modeled as a straight line). This score falling on the straight line can be referred to as her **predicted value** of locus of control, because quite literally it is what her value of locus of control would be if we calculated it from the straight-line equation (Eq. 5.1), knowing her value of cultural consonance. The difference between this predicted value (shown as an x on the regression line in Figure 5.6) and the mean for each person can be thought of as the **explained variation.** Why? Because we have accounted for that portion of the difference between a person's locus of control and the mean locus of control by taking into account cultural consonance (as I said in the last chapter, we know where to put that variation).

Then, there's a chunk of information left unexplained: the difference between a person's actual data point and the predicted data point that falls on the straight line. This we can refer to as the **unexplained variation,** because we frankly have no idea why his actual locus of control still deviates from what we would guess it is based on his cultural consonance. I have indicated

FIGURE 5.6 Explained variation between predicted values of locus of control
scores on the regression line and the mean of locus of control scores

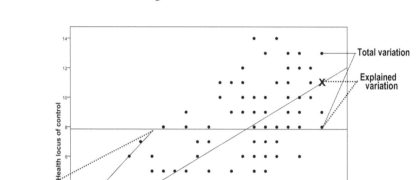

the difference between the predicted data point and the actual data point in
Figure 5.7.

Remember that we are squaring and summing all of these values, so that
we are dealing with the differences represented by these concepts in a general
sense, getting rid of the positive and negative values. We can now offer an
answer to the question of whether knowing a person's cultural consonance
is really doing us any good. We can look at the explained variation as a
proportion of the total variation. In this case, that proportion is 37%; that
is, the sum of the squared differences between the predicted locus of control
scores lying on the straight line and the mean locus of control scores, divided
by the sum of the squared differences between the actual data points and the
mean locus of control scores, is 37%. We have "explained" 37% of the total
variation in locus of control scores by taking into account cultural consonance
(you will also run into people who would say that we have explained 37% of
the variance—variation and variance tend to get used interchangeably here).

Another way to think about this is that we have "explained" 37% of the
distance between an individual's actual locus of control score and the mean for

FIGURE 5.7 Unexplained variation between observed locus of control scores and predicted locus of control scores

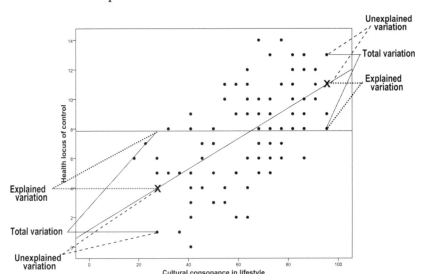

the sample by knowing her cultural consonance. The proportion of explained variation translates into a correlation coefficient of $r = .61$. The proportion of the variation explained in a dependent variable by an independent variable is the square of the correlation coefficient; hence the correlation coefficient is the square root of the proportion of variance explained. Also, it should be obvious that the maximum value that a correlation can have is 1.00, because you cannot explain more than 100% of the variation in a variable. So the correlation coefficient varies between 0 and 1.0, indicating how well the observed association of two variable conforms to a straight-line model.

Next we can ask the same sort of question about the reliability or stability of this finding over different hypothetical samples of 100 persons drawn from Ribeirão Preto. If we did this study 1,000 times over, how likely are we to get a correlation of $r = .61$ if that correlation is actually zero? In other words, since we did this study only one time, are we the unluckiest people in the world, getting what looks like an interesting finding purely by chance? Think again of a hypothetical distribution, this time of correlation coefficients. If the correlation between cultural consonance and locus of control is really zero, and if we rerun this study 1,000 times, mostly we are going to get correlations slightly different from, but clustered around, zero. Once in a while, however, we will get, by chance, a really big correlation coefficient that sits out on the tail of the distribution. It turns out that if the association were truly zero, a finding of a correlation of $r = .61$ would be 7.585 standard error units away from the hypothetical mean of zero, or way out on the tail of such a distribution. This situation would be likely to happen considerably less than 1 in 1,000 times, or a probability value of $p < .001$. Could it be baloney? Yes, but it's not *likely* to be baloney.

Is 37% of the variation explained respectable? Should we be happy with this finding? This is a somewhat complicated question that I'm going to defer for the next chapter. Right now I want us to think about the correlation coefficient a little bit more. Don't freak out, but I'm going to introduce here an actual equation for the Pearson correlation coefficient (note the indefinite article *an*; there are different ways to calculate it):

EQUATION 5.3

$$r = \frac{\sum_i (x_i - \bar{x})(y_i - \bar{y})}{\sqrt{\sum_i (x_i - \bar{x})^2}\ \sqrt{\sum_i (y_i - \bar{y})^2}}$$

Actually, pretty much everything in this equation ought to be familiar. On top, or in the numerator, within each set of parentheses we are subtracting the mean for a variable from each observation, just as we did in calculating the standard deviation for each variable. There are a couple of catches, however. In the first place, we are not squaring the difference, so we are retaining the negative numbers. In the second place, we are doing it for each variable. So for each person, we subtract the mean of locus of control from his score for locus of control, and we subtract the mean for cultural consonance from his score for cultural consonance. We are doing this simultaneously. Finally, we multiply those deviations.

Think about what that numerator is going to do under different situations. If, in general, people in the sample are far away from the mean for locus of control at the same time that they are far away from the mean for cultural consonance, that number in the numerator is going to be big, and it's going to be a positive number. It will be a positive number because, if people are lower than the mean on both variables, multiplying them together gives you a positive number, and if people are higher than the mean on both variables, multiplying them together still gives you a positive number. If, however, people tend to be above the mean on one variable but below the mean on the other variable, one deviation will tend to be positive while the other deviation will tend to be negative, so you'll end up with a negative number.

I illustrate the notion of a negative or inverse correlation in Figure 5.8 with some data I recently collected in Brazil. This figure shows the correlation of cultural consonance and symptoms of psychological distress. The hypothesis here is that the more you fulfill the shared expectations in your society, the better you feel; so your psychological distress goes down as cultural consonance increases. And the actual data are consistent with this simple linear model ($r = -.57$).

Going back to equation 5.3, we ask what would happen if people tended to be very different from the mean on one variable but not very different on the other. In this case, the magnitude of the product in the numerator would be fairly small.

Finally, what about the bottom half of the equation, the denominator? As you can see, we are coming close to calculating the standard deviation for

---

FIGURE 5.8 Inverse correlation between psychological distress and cultural consonance

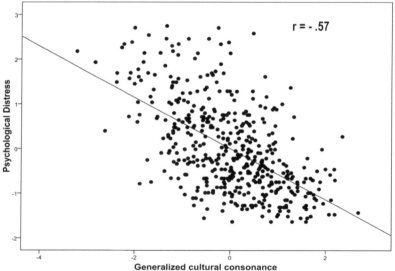

each of the variables; we're just not dividing by the total sample size, and we are multiplying them together. The denominator of the equation represents the total variation that I discussed earlier. What the denominator does in this way of calculating the correlation coefficient is to, in effect, standardize the coefficient, in a way analogous to the z-scores we talked about earlier, except that in this case the correlation coefficient can vary only between 0.00 and 1.00, and it can take a positive or negative sign. The closer you are to 1.0, the more of the variation you are able to "explain," and the direction of the association can be positive or negative, as shown in Figures 5.7 and 5.8.

Going back to our earlier question—how well does the straight line function as a model for our observed data: the correlation coefficient can help to answer that. The larger the correlation coefficient, the better the straight line does as a representation for our data. Is $r = .61$ a good representation? Again, this is a complicated question, and one to which we will return later. For now I would have to answer "yes"; it looks pretty good to me.

Another thing to keep in mind about the correlation coefficient is that it is **symmetric**. What this means is that you get the same correlation coefficient if you think about plotting locus of control on the x-axis and cultural consonance on the y-axis. It doesn't change. We will see later that other kinds of coefficients don't have this particular property, which means that the correlation coefficient can be thought of as simply describing shared variation or variance between two variables.

SUMMARY

The great methodologists from psychology, Jacob and Patricia Cohen, entitled their textbook *Applied Multiple Regression/Correlation Analysis for the Behavioral Sciences* (1975); this is an old edition, but it happens to be my favorite. In titling their book this way, they emphasized that correlation and linear regression are essentially the same thing. I have followed their thinking and have introduced the correlation coefficient here in the context of **linear regression**. In statistical parlance, that simple little straight line is a linear regression. What we did was regress locus of control on cultural consonance. The underlying model is the straight line, and the measure of the goodness of fit of the straight line to the data is the correlation coefficient.

You will run into lots of discussions of the correlation coefficient and lots of uses of the correlation coefficient that have no reference whatsoever to the underlying linear regression model. That's fine, because the correlation coefficient is a wonderfully flexible tool that we can put to use in a whole variety of ways. At its foundation, however, is the linear regression model. In fact, in much (really most) of statistical modeling we think about the world in terms of straight lines (and more about that later).

Quantification in Ethnographic Research

Some Additional Thoughts on the 5 Things You Need to Know about Statistics

I have presented the 5 things you need to know about statistics: measures of central tendency, especially the arithmetic mean; measures of dispersion, especially the standard deviation; the logic of statistical significance testing using the chi-square; the logic of statistical significance testing using the analysis of variance; and the correlation coefficient. We are now going to start meditating a bit on the meaning of this all, and especially on some of the complications involved in thinking statistically. In this chapter I introduce some additional considerations relevant to our previous discussion: levels of statistical significance, variance explained, and the myriad of statistical tests that one can use.

LEVELS OF STATISTICAL SIGNIFICANCE

You now know precisely what "$p < .05$" means. It means that your test statistic, whether it be a chi-square value, an F-ratio, or a correlation coefficient, sits out on the tail of a distribution that has been calculated for that statistic under the assumption that there is no relationship between the two variables being evaluated. If you find that a test statistic of a certain magnitude, just that one time that you have carried out your study, sits way out on that tail, you have to wonder how you could have been so (un)lucky to have gotten that result purely by chance. Since in that distribution that result would occur infrequently by chance, it is reasonable to infer that in fact there really is an association between the two variables.

But . . . how "infrequent" must that result be? The standard way of evaluating this potential frequency of chance occurrences—or statistical significance—is to say that .05, or 5 chances out of 100, or 1 chance in 20, is a reasonable level. Why? There is actually not a good answer to that question. Of course there is the historical precedent, which in this case means that Sir Ronald Fisher (1925) recommended the .05 level. There is, however, no logical reason for selecting the .05 level of statistical significance.

Statistical significance varies in relation to several things. You might have heard of something called **power analysis.** This refers to your ability to actually detect a statistically significant relationship within a sample of data. Power analysis is based on the fact that your ability to detect a statistically significant relationship varies in relation to both the actual strength of the relationship that you are trying to observe and the sample size (see Weller 2015 for a useful and accessible introduction to power analysis). Statistical analysis is in part all about estimation, or what I have often referred to in this book as guessing, and then evaluating your confidence in that guess. When examining the association between cultural consonance and locus of control, for example, we can imagine that in some pristine social system devoid of messy noise and complications, there is a "true" correlation between these variables. We are, however, stuck with messy, noisy, and complicated social systems within which we are trying to get a glimpse (or an estimate) of this association. What I mean by noise and messiness are things like your respondents only half paying attention to you during the interview and not really answering the question being asked (this would be measurement error). Or your sample of respondents not really having the full representative range of socioeconomic variation in the community, because, for some odd reason, you just don't feel like going into that neighborhood to interview people where the drug traffickers have twitchy 14-year-olds with AK-47s posted as lookouts (a restricted range of variation can lead to an under-estimate of a correlation). Or you decide to interview respondents within a certain age range, knowing that you are missing part of the variation, because that will help you when it comes to other variables in your study (which is what I did in my first study of blood pressure; Dressler 1982). These (and many others) are the kinds of factors that introduce noise into the data we collect. When the "true" correlation between two variables is rather large, we can more easily get a glimpse of it despite all the noise and messiness of the real world.

Sample size is the other main factor affecting statistical power. Think back to the example of the correlation coefficient given in the preceding chapter. We get a certain result ($r = .61$ in that case), and in our thought experiment we come up with a theoretical distribution of 1,000 replications of that study, in which the expected value of the correlation is $r = .00$. If that is the expected correlation, how likely are we to get $r = .61$ purely by chance? Not very likely, the level of statistical significance being $p < .001$. We can get to that p-value by calculating the standard error of the distribution of the 1,000 hypothetical correlations and seeing where the observed correlation falls in the distribution, which we do by dividing the correlation by the standard error. Part of the way we get to estimate that standard error is by using the actual sample size that we have. If you have a relatively small sample size, that standard error is going to be larger, because the distribution will tend to be more spread out. As the sample size increases, the standard error will become relatively smaller, because you are getting a better picture of the overall distribution. So, as your sample size increases, you are better able to estimate the statistically significant relationship, if it is really there.

What this all means is that, right off the bat, when you are thinking about levels of statistical significance, you have to think about them in terms of both your ability to estimate the association and your sample size. There is no magic that says $p < .05$ is always the key to what is important in your data. And remember that what you are trying to do is to figure out how much confidence you have in your results. That's what it is all about. A finding with a $p < .05$, or a $p < .10$ or a $p < .001$, doesn't mean that the finding is absolutely "true"; your theoretical and ethnographic acumen are what enable you to interpret your results in that sense. The level of statistical significance only leads you to be able to state your findings with greater or lesser confidence, and I mean this literally. When you are at a national meeting, standing in front of a room full of your peers and giving a paper, how confidently are you going to assert that you "know" that there is an association between, for example, cultural consonance and locus of control?

This focus on levels of confidence, as opposed to levels of statistical significance, has been observed in different ways in the social science literature. For example, the distinguished sociologist Ronald Kessler has published papers in which he notes statistical associations that are about twice their standard error (Kessler & Neighbors 1986). This situation would actually mean, if you thought about it in this way, that these associations are significant at the $p < .05$ level. But what Kessler is emphasizing by doing this is his confidence that these are all, at least, statistically reliable findings. They are unlikely to have occurred by chance. What do they really mean? That is for theory and ethnographic insight to answer.

Another, perhaps even notorious, example of downplaying the importance of p-values was provided by the epidemiologist and biostatistician Kenneth Rothman when he was the editor of the American Journal of Public Health (Fidler et al. 2004). He forbade the reporting of levels of statistical significance. Instead, he required that the actual confidence intervals be reported. As you now know, if you estimate the standard error of a coefficient, you can calculate the upper and lower limits within which that coefficient will vary in repeated samples from the same population. The $p < .05$ level of statistical significance means, in the case of a correlation coefficient, that, in 95% of hypothetical replications of a study, upper and lower limits will not include zero. Rothman, rather sensibly, thought that it would be more informative for authors to report the actual confidence intervals. So, from this perspective, our finding of a significant association between cultural consonance and locus of control would be reported as $r = .61$ $(.47, .72)$. Or, in 95% of repeated samples from Ribeirão Preto, the correlation of cultural consonance and locus of control is likely to vary from as low as $r = .47$ to as high as $r = .72$.

My point here is not to be prescriptive in what you should do (although I really like Kessler's way of thinking about this). My point is for you not to become fixated on p-values. They mean only what they mean, and nothing more. A statistically significant coefficient of whatever kind is simply a few times larger than its own standard error. It means, in other words, that it is likely a stable finding in that community. Whatever else it means is for you to figure out.

VARIANCE EXPLAINED

One of my pet peeves involves sitting in a lecture and listening to what I think is a really interesting paper full of fascinating results, and some guy next to me leans over and asserts, in a slightly condescending tone of voice, "Well, she didn't explain much of the variance, did she?" Another version of this is "Well, that's not a very large correlation, is it?" As you now know, these are related comments, in that the square of the Pearson correlation coefficient expresses the amount of variance shared by two variables.

Now, don't get me wrong, I like to explain whopping amounts of variance as much as the next guy; however, there are lots of obstacles out there to explaining large amounts of variance and to estimating coefficients that appear to have large effects. The issue of variance explained hearkens back to my discussion of power analysis. The data we collect are often, and perhaps inherently, noisy. One of the most thoughtful discussions of this situation in the philosophy of science comes from the critical realist philosopher Roy Bhaskar (1989). Bhaskar points out that the great advantage of experimental sciences—such as biology, chemistry, and physics—is that practitioners of these sciences can create artificially closed systems in their laboratories, and their experimental observations are generated within these closed systems. For example, to observe the behavior of some particle, the physicist can create an artificial vacuum within his or her laboratory, getting rid of the pesky effects of friction within an atmosphere. Social scientists, in contrast, operate in inherently open systems. For anthropologists, these are usually communities. Even for experimental social scientists, who randomly assign human subjects to different experimental conditions, those human subjects are carrying all sorts of uncontrollable baggage with them into the laboratory that can only partially be randomized away. So there are lots of influences on our respondents that we just can't get rid of, and they can sometimes influence the associations that we are trying to understand.

Yet we are taught that, for example, the correlation coefficient can vary between 0.00 and 1.00 (and, of course, it can take a positive or negative sign). The closer to 1.00 that correlation is, the stronger it is and the more variance explained. The problem is that, like normal distributions, correlations in nature are subject to all sorts of influences that lead them to fall short of their theoretical ideal. To illustrate this situation, think back to our example of the association between neighborhood of residence and locus of control. We dichotomized neighborhood into lower and higher SES areas, and we dichotomized locus of control into external and internal. It turns out that there is a correlation coefficient—called the **phi coefficient**—that can estimate the correlation between two dichotomous variables. And, it turns out that the phi coefficient is actually a familiar Pearson correlation coefficient when the two variables are measured as dichotomies instead of continuous variables (I'll discuss this more later).

In our example phi = .36, or the higher the SES of the neighborhood you live in, the more likely you are to have an internal locus of control. Is this correlation good, bad, or indifferent? For starters, the correlation is statistically significant, which is good and a good thing to know, but the statistical significance tells us only that the correlation is unlikely to have occurred by chance. Is the value of .36 worth paying attention to? No doubt there are some who would read this in a paper and scoff, thinking that .36 is pretty far from 1.0, hence not very important. But would it even be possible to achieve a value of 1.0 in these data? Turns out that the answer is "no." Looking back to our example in Chapter 3, we see that neither neighborhood of residence nor locus of control is evenly distributed. In fact, locus of control departs pretty substantially from an even distribution, with 57% answering questions in a way consistent with an external locus of control and 43% answering in a way consistent with an internal locus of control. This departure from an even distribution in each variable affects the upper bound of a correlation that could exist in these data.

In Table 6.1, I have reproduced a portion of a table that first appeared in a paper by Whitt (1983). The rows of the table represent the distribution of one dichotomous variable in a 2 x 2 contingency table, so the row labeled "30%" indicates that this variable would have a 30–70 split in terms of "high versus low," or "present versus absent," or however that variable might be conceptualized. The columns of the table represent the same thing for the second variable in your 2 x 2 contingency table. In the cells of the table the maximum possible value of the phi-coefficient is given for a contingency table in which each of the two variables has those marginal distributions. Note that when the distribution of one variable is the same as the distribution of the other variable, the phi-coefficient can reach 1.0; when, however, one or the other variables departs from an even distribution, or is different from the other variable, the theoretical maximum of the coefficient is actually less than 1.0. When one variable has a 50-50 split on the dichotomy, and the other variable has a 30-70 split, the maximum value of the phi-coefficient is phi = .65.

Returning to our own example, the phi = .36 association starts to look a little different in this light. With the 60-40 split in locus of control, and the not-quite-even split in neighborhood of residence, the maximum possible phi-coefficient you could find in this table would be less than 1.0, and the phi = .36 might actually be about 50% of the maximum possible correlation. In other words, we might be explaining a substantial portion of the variation that it is theoretically possible to explain in these data.

TABLE 6.1 Maximum possible phi/correlation coefficient for dichotomous variables with different distributions (adapted from Whitt 1983)

		PROPORTIONAL DISTRIBUTION OF ONE VARIABLE IN A 2 X 2 CROSSTABULATION*			
		30%	40%	50%	60%
PROPORTIONAL DISTRIBUTION OF THE OTHER VARIABLE IN A 2 X 2 CROSSTABULATION*	30%	1.00	.80	.65	.53
	40%	.80	1.00	.82	.67
	50%	.65	.82	1.00	.82
	60%	.53	.67	.82	1.00

*Note: Each variable is a dichotomy. "30%" indicates that, for that variable, 30% of the cases are "present" while 70% are "absent." "40%" indicates that, for that variable, 40% of the cases are "present" while 60% are "absent," etc.

This example generalizes to variables measured on a continuum. Any departure from normality in the distribution of one variable is going to reduce the theoretical maximum of the correlation it can have with any other variable. And things get even a little more complicated. **Reliability** in the measurement of a variable refers to the degree to which that measurement, applied under basically the same conditions to the same set of respondents who have not undergone any significant change in circumstances, returns the same values. A simple way of assessing reliability is to administer a measurement—such as the locus of control scale—to a group of respondents, and then a week later give them the same scale. You calculate a correlation between the two sets of values and you get what is called their "test-retest" reliability. For the sake of argument, let's say that reliability = .85. Why is it not a perfect 1.0? Remember that we live in a messy, noisy world. Languages are imperfect vehicles for capturing the psychological disposition we are trying to measure with the scale of locus of control, and a well-meaning and attentive respondent can think about the meaning of a word differently from one week to the next. Or respondents have headaches one week but they didn't the week before. One or two respondents broke up with their significant others and are feeling bummed out. Overall there has been no change in the sample of respondents, but stuff happens. There's noise. The measure of reliability tells us, roughly, how much noise there is or, perhaps more accurately, how well our measurement does in cutting through the inherent noise in the world to capture the information (sometimes referred to as the **signal**) that we are trying to capture.

By definition, the noise in one variable is not going to correlate with the noise in another variable, because it's, well, noise. It's not real, systematic, causally generated variation. It's only the real, systematic, causally generated variation in one variable that can connect to the same in another variable. More formally, the correlation between two variables is generally smaller than the product of their reliabilities. If two variables have reliabilities of .9 (which, by the way, is quite good), their maximum possible correlation turns out to be .81, not 1.0.

At this point those of you with a relatively lower tolerance for ambiguity might be ready to throw up your hands and shout that none of this statistics stuff is any good if it's all so contingent on a bunch of other stuff (which often we don't know, like the true reliabilities of our variables). That, of course, is not the moral of the story. As noisy, messy, and contingent as the world is, thinking numerically in this way still gives us a clear model for helping us to understand the world, and it gives us a way to evaluate our confidence in our statements that does not rely on our subjective states. The real moral to this story is that you cannot substitute formulae or formulaic ways of thinking for judgment. When you are looking at a correlation coefficient, think about it in the overall context of the research. Use your judgment.

ALL THOSE STATISTICAL TESTS

One thing that confuses beginners and more seasoned practitioners alike is the welter of statistical tests that are available, both tests of statistical difference (such as the *t*-test and ANOVA) and tests of association (the correlation coefficient). How do you know what to do? The classic approach is to base decisions on measurement level. At the beginning of this book I noted the four classic levels of measurement: nominal, ordinal, interval, and ratio. But then I backed off and went with two levels: categorical and continuous. This approach was based on the notion that, although a measure may be strictly speaking ordinal, in that it really ranks respondents only along a continuum, if you get a sufficient number of ranks into the mix, that ordinal scale can begin to behave like an interval scale. Our own well-worn scale of health locus of control is an example. The scale ranges from 0 to 14, and there is no reason to argue that a person who has a score of 8 is exactly twice as much in terms of internal locus of control than the person with a score of 4. Yet, at the same time, the distribution of the scale scores looks pretty normal-like in a histogram, and 14 divisions seems pretty good. So, I feel comfortable treating it as a continuous scale with "interval-like" properties and hence using fairly advanced statistics with it (see Dressler, Balieiro, Ribeiro, & Dos Santos 2007; Dressler, Balieiro, & Dos Santos 1999).

Complications ensue when you cannot reasonably make such assumptions—that is, when you cannot treat your measures as continuous in this sense. Many of the confusing number of statistical tests are there to relieve you of having to make certain assumptions, in particular, two: an interval level of measurement and a normally distributed variable. These are the basic assumptions required to use what are called **parametric** statistics such as the analysis of variance and the Pearson correlation coefficient (and of course, the analysis of variance relates one nominal and one continuous variable, whereas correlations relate two continuous variables). **Nonparametric** versions of these tests (specifically **Kruskal-Wallis one-way analysis of variance by ranks** and the **Spearman rank-order correlation coefficient**) are to be applied when you cannot reasonably make the assumption that your variables at least approximate an interval-like continuous variation.

Again, the long and the short of it is your judgment. I don't think we should be scared away from using more powerful parametric statistics when we can, because the data-analytic payoffs are considerable. At the same time, we certainly do not want to be basing our statements about the world on a piece of data analysis that is, at best, suspect and, at worst, meaningless garbage. My own personal solution to this problem is to analyze my data in several different ways. Virtually any article of mine that makes it into print has been analyzed in several different ways, with of course only one version of that analysis seeing the light of day. I use this approach to convince myself that I'm not fooling myself into believing something about my data that is not true. If I get essentially the same answer in several different ways, the associations in the data are sufficiently robust for me to believe they are real. Approaching your data in this way simply requires that you develop a familiarity with the various ways of examining statistical associations that make relatively fewer demands on the nature of those data. (See, for example, Jim Leeper's comprehensive guide to statistical tests, reproduced at http://bama.ua.edu/~jleeper/627/choosestat.html and http://www.ats.ucla.edu/stat/mult_pkg/whatstat/).

At this point, however, I want to turn to a slightly different but related idea. In Chapter 4 we discussed the analysis of variance, and at the end of the chapter I noted that the t-test for the difference in means between two groups is a special case of ANOVA. Figure 4.7 shows an error bar graph for the difference in mean locus of control between lower and higher SES neighborhoods in Ribeirão Preto. Table 6.2 gives the output from SPSS for the t-test, showing that the mean difference between the two groups—2.615— is unlikely to have occurred by chance ($t = 4.542$, $df = 98$, $p < .001$).

Think about the error bar graph in Figure 4.7, with the straight line connecting the mean locus of control for the lower SES groups and the mean locus of control for the higher SES groups. Where else have we encountered a straight line like this? Think about the line that we drew in Figure 5.3 to characterize the association between cultural consonance and locus of control. Remember that we used a linear regression analysis to "find" that line, in the sense that there is only one best-fitting line to those data points, that line being one that minimizes the sum of the squared deviations of data points from that line. Well, what if we did the same thing here? What if we fed locus of control and the dichotomous indicator of neighborhood of residence into a linear regression? Actually, this is not as crazy as it might sound, since a dichotomy, especially if it is properly coded (in this case the lower SES neighborhoods are given a code of 0, and the upper SES neighborhoods are given a code of 1, which is called **effects coding** in regression parlance), acts as an interval variable—because there is only one interval! So, you do a linear regression analysis in SPSS, with the neighborhood dichotomous variable as the independent variable and health locus of control as the dependent variable, and you get the following linear regression equation:

HLOC = 6.569 + 2.615 * Neighborhood.

The thing about a linear regression, or straight line, model like this is that you need to actually plug values in to see what is going on. This model says that, to estimate (guess) the HLOC score for a particular neighborhood, you have to multiply the indicator value for that neighborhood times 2.615 and add that value to 6.569. Since we have used a value of 0 to represent the lower SES neighborhoods, when we multiply that times 2.615 we get 0, which means that the estimated mean HLOC for the lower SES neighborhoods is 6.569. And, in Table 6.2, the mean of locus of control from the lower SES neighborhood from our t-test is 6.5686 (SPSS uses slightly different rules

TABLE 6.2 *t*-test for the difference in locus of control between low and high SES neighborhoods

		GROUP STATISTICS			
	Neighborhood	*N*	Mean	Std. Deviation	Std. Error Mean
HEALTH LOCUS OF CONTROL	Low SES	51	6.5686	3.02823	0.42404
	High SES	49	9.1837	2.71319	0.38760

	INDEPENDENT SAMPLES TEST				
	t-test for Equality of Means				
HEALTH LOCUS OF CONTROL	*t*	*df*	Sig. (2-tailed)	Mean Difference	Std. Error Difference
	−4.542	98	.000	−2.61505	.57576

for rounding off output from one program to the next). From the linear regression, to estimate mean HLOC for higher SES neighborhoods, we have to multiply 1 (the value we used to represent the higher SES neighborhoods) times 2.615 to get 2.615 and then add that to 6.589, for a value of 9.184. Table 6.2 shows that the mean value of locus of control for upper SES neighborhoods is 9.1837 (again, different rules for rounding off the output). And, finally, testing the statistical significance of the linear regression coefficient—which is the slope, or 2.615—we get $t = 4.542$ ($p < .001$). And of course, you will have noted already that 2.615 happens to be the mean difference between lower and higher SES neighborhoods. In other words, we get exactly the same results from a linear regression analysis as we do from a simple *t*-test.

We can see a similar result in the analysis of variance we did in Chapter 4. Table 4.1 gives that ANOVA for the association of education and locus of control. We can use regression analysis to look at this analysis by converting education to what are called **dummy variables.** A dummy variable takes a simple ordinal scale such as education, consisting of only three ordered categories—primary, secondary, or advanced education—and converts them to a couple of dichotomous variables. Literally, we create a variable in which if you have a secondary education you get a code of 1, and if you don't have a secondary education (obviously meaning you have either a primary or advanced education), you get a code of 0. Then, if you have an advanced education you get a code of 1, and if you don't have an advanced education (meaning again that you have either a primary or secondary education), you get a code of 0. You then put these variables into a regression analysis, and you get this:

HLOC = 6.7 + 2.36 * secondary education + 3.18*advanced education.

(see the next chapter for a discussion of **multivariate linear regression,** that is, more than one independent variable). If we substitute values as we did in the previous example, for people who have a primary school education, people's codes for the secondary and advanced education variables will be 0, and hence their predicted locus of control score will be 6.7. Check Table 4.1, and you will see that 6.7 is in fact the mean of locus of control for people with a primary school education. For people with a secondary education, since their code for that variable is 1, to get their HLOC score we add 6.7 and 2.36 for a value of 9.06, which again is the mean that we see in Table 5.1. Finally, people with an advanced education would have a predicted value of HLOC of 6.7 + 3.18, or 9.88, which yet again is the same as in Table 4.1. The F-ratio from the regression analysis is 12.75 ($p < .001$), which is also exactly the same as in Table 4.1.

What's the point of all this? Well, I'm hoping to convince you that, in conventional statistical analysis, our model of the world is a straight line. Yes, there are numerous different kinds of statistical tests out there, but, in general, what it all boils down to is that we are using a straight line as a model for how things go together in the world.

Let me hasten to add that there are all sorts of ways of taking into account the possibilities of curvilinear associations and other more complex models, such as the possibility that the degree of association between two variables changes depending on the context within which a person lives (this is *moderation*, or an *interaction effect*). At the same time, to envision these more complex kinds of associations, we generally modify the basic straight-line model in various ways. But I think that it is worth thinking about our statistical analyses in terms of the basic underlying model for a couple of reasons. The first is not to get bogged down in your thinking while learning this or that statistical test. Rather, keep your eyes on the prize in terms of where you are heading, which is to understand how events and circumstances in the world affect other events and circumstances. Having to learn when to use a Mann-Whitney U-test instead of a standard t-test doesn't mean you are doing something remarkably different. It just means that no matter how hard you plug your nose and squint at your data in various ways, the continuous dependent variable you have just refuses to approximate normality close enough to use the t-test.

The second reason to think about statistics in terms of the basic underlying model is to emphasize the fact that we are trying to see how well our data can be described in terms of a straight line (again, with the proviso that there are all sorts of ways of using these basic methods to get after curvilinear associations, moderating effects, threshold effects, and others). It is a model, not some kind of timeless, essential, eternal truth. Models are cool. Why do engineers build little model airplanes and stick them in wind tunnels before they go out and build multiton behemoths? Why did Niels Bohr use the Copernican conceptualization of the solar system as a model for the atom? Why is artificial intelligence sometimes used as a model for biological consciousness? Because models are good to think with. Using conventional statistical models for our data can help us to think about implications of those data that we may never have thought of otherwise. And in doing so we can actually place some intervals in our confidence around the kinds of inferences and interpretations being offered. So, yes, a straight line is a pretty simple model, and, yes, it can be incredibly useful.

SUMMARY

My aim in this chapter has been to consider a few questions that can be perplexing for students who are first encountering statistical analysis. These include the question of level of statistical significance; variance explained, or, more generally, the magnitude of statistical associations; and the myriad of statistical tests that can be encountered. None of these are cut-and-dried issues. Thinking about each requires reflection and principled judgment. And by absorbing the 5 things you need to know about statistics, you will be in a good position to begin that reflection and make those principled judgments.

Three Analyses Extending the Concept of Correlation

I wrote at the outset of this book that absorbing the 5 things you need to know about statistics would enable you to immediately incorporate some numeric thinking into your fieldwork, thus achieving the anthropological ideal of mixed-methods, qualitative-quantitative research. More important, however, understanding these 5 things will better position you to go on and understand some of the more powerful statistical models available. This is the gravy.

I am not going to present anything approaching an exhaustive overview of statistical models that can be used. Bernard (2011) and Handwerker and Borgatti (2014) provide just such grand tours. Rather, in this chapter I delve into three models and their application to research questions in some detail. Furthermore, these three models apply everything that we have covered thus far, and they are based primarily on the correlation coefficient. Each model uses the properties of the correlation coefficient in somewhat different ways to answer questions of enduring interest in anthropology.

MULTIPLE REGRESSION ANALYSIS

Anyone with a passing familiarity with my work will know that multiple regression analysis is a big favorite of mine. The basic reason for this is that in my research in biocultural medical anthropology, I almost always focus on a health outcome; blood pressure, body mass, immune function, and depressive symptoms are all outcomes or dependent variables that have been a focus of my research. The basic research strategy has been to isolate and measure a cultural variable, such as cultural consonance, and then to examine how it is associated with health outcomes while controlling for other factors known to influence that outcome. For example, it is well known that increasing age and increasing body mass are both associated with increasing blood pressure. Therefore, if I want to determine how cultural consonance influences blood pressure, I have to examine its association after I have statistically "controlled for" age and body mass. Multiple regression analysis is ideally suited to this research strategy.

As I presented it in Chapter 5, regression and correlation are two sides of the same coin. Regression gives you the straight line; correlation tells you how well your data conform to that straight line. Again, according to high school algebra, that straight line is

EQUATION 6.1

$$Y = a + bX,$$

where Y is the dependent variable (such as blood pressure) and X is the independent variable (such as cultural consonance). The point at which the line crosses the vertical axis is given by the constant a, and b is the slope of the line (called a **regression coefficient** in regression lingo—and, by the way, the numerator for the calculation of the regression coefficient is the same as the numerator for the correlation coefficient) or the amount by which X has to be weighted in order to predict Y, adding in the constant. The beauty of this simple linear regression is that it can be extended:

EQUATION 6.2

$$Y = a + b_1 X_1 + b_2 X_2 + b_3 X_3 + b_n X_n.$$

There are some rather complicated geometric models for thinking about multiple regression, but just looking at the algebra is pretty straightforward. Each X or independent variable contributes a little bit more information to the prediction of (or approximation of or guessing of) the dependent variable Y, which improves the fit of the straight line to the data. Therefore, adding independent variables to the equation improves the model. (Of course you can't go on ad infinitum, although some econometricians seem to; there's a limit on the number of independent variables you can introduce relative to your sample size. Many people suggest 6 times as many cases as you have independent variables in your equation.)

One of the remarkable things about a multiple regression model is that once you have introduced a variable into the equation, it has been controlled for. For example, if X_1 and X_2 in Equation 6.2 were age and body mass, respectively, and X_3 was cultural consonance, then the slope b_3 would be the amount of change in Y (or blood pressure) for every change per unit of cultural consonance, controlling for age and body mass. Literally, the regression coefficient for cultural consonance would be the effect of cultural consonance on blood pressure *as if* everyone were the same age and had the same body mass. The formulae for understanding how other variables are controlled for can be a little complicated, involving **partial regression coefficients** and **partial correlation coefficients** (the term *partial* here refers to controlling for something). But looking at the regression equation can give you some insight. Imagine that we are just using age to predict blood pressure. You will have two values: the observed value of blood pressure and the value predicted from age. Since age is not a perfect predictor of blood pressure, there will be a difference between the actual value and the value predicted from age (something we saw graphically in the chapter on the correlation coefficient). This is called a *residual,* because it is the value of blood pressure left over when you have taken account of how well age can be used to estimate the value of blood pressure. Then, when body mass goes into the equation, one can try to estimate the residual value of blood pressure, or what is left over after age has done all the explaining it can. What is left over in blood pressure is, by definition, independent of age. Once body mass has explained all it can, then what is left over can perhaps be accounted for by cultural consonance, and so on. This notion of a residual value will come in handy when we are considering a lot of different statistical models.

As an example of the use of multiple regression analysis, let's again look at the correlation of cultural consonance and locus of control. One thing we might like to do here is to simply control for age and gender, not for any strong theoretical reason but because it is possible that they might be correlated or confounded with other variables in the analysis, and it would be good just to clear away some of the noise, if it's there. A more pressing variable to control for might be family income. Remember that the specific measure of cultural consonance used here is cultural consonance in lifestyle, or the degree to which people accumulate the material goods and engage in the leisure time activities that are collectively thought (as verified by cultural consensus analysis, discussed shortly) to be important for "having a good life." Given the correlation of $r = .61$ between cultural consonance and locus of control, we can reasonably argue that the degree of culturally defined success in life that individuals enjoy enhances their sense of agency in their own lives (and, of course, it could be argued that the influence runs in the other direction, but we'll discuss that later). A reasonable objection to this argument, however, would be a simple economic resources argument. That is, people who have higher income might have both the opportunity and the access to a culturally consonant lifestyle, *and* they might have a stronger sense of internal control and agency. This line of reasoning suggests that the correlation of cultural consonance and locus of control is **spurious**—it occurs simply because both variables are correlated with income, that is, it only appears that cultural consonance and locus of control are correlated, because each is correlated with income. So, it would seem prudent to enter income into the analysis (income is measured here as the number of minimum salaries per month that working members of the household earn, a government-set value that Brazilians use to describe their incomes).

Table 7.1 shows the results of the multiple regression analysis. It also illustrates something else: you can control the entry of variables into a multiple regression model in order to see how the model changes when variables are added or subtracted. In this case we start with the simplest model that just has age and sex in it (which is a rather boring model to boot, given that neither age nor sex has any association with HLOC). In the second model, income is added to the equation, and, as suspected, it has a substantial association with locus of control. The number given in the table—.46—is called a **partial regression coefficient.** It is the *b* in the equation for the straight line, or how much locus of control changes with each increment in income. It is partial because it is controlling for age and sex. Note from the placement of the asterisks that we can test directly the statistical significance of the regression coefficient or slope. There is another interesting thing about this regression coefficient: it is **standardized.** Remember in Chapter 2 when I introduced the idea of a *z*-score?—that is, a score that represents a person's value on some variable like locus of control as relative to the mean and the standard deviation. The standardized regression coefficient is calculated as if all the variables have been converted to *z*-scores. The upshot is that the

TABLE 7.1 Multiple linear regression of locus of control on covariates, income, and cultural consonance

VARIABLES	MODEL 1	MODEL 2	MODEL 3
AGE	-.03	-.12	-.19*
SEX	-.04	-.12	.02
INCOME	--	.46**	.14
CULTURAL CONSONANCE	--		.57**
MULTIPLE R	.05	.45**	.64**
MULTIPLE R^2	.01	.20	.41

standardized regression coefficients are comparable from one variable to the next.

Look what happens when cultural consonance enters the equation. The association of income and locus of control drops to, in essence, zero (it ceases to be statistically significant, so you can't really tell the difference between that coefficient and zero), and the entire effect is absorbed by cultural consonance. How does this work? Looking at the bivariate correlations, income and locus of control are correlated at $r = .41$ ($p < .001$). Cultural consonance and locus of control are correlated at $r = .61$ ($p < .001$), and, not surprisingly, income and locus of control are correlated at $r = .53$ ($p < .001$). So locus of control is either an outcome of both of the independent variables together, and their correlation simply means that they share some of the variance explained in locus of control because they are correlated. Or, it means that one of the two variables of income and cultural consonance is correlated with locus of control simply by virtue of the fact that income and cultural consonance are correlated. In other words, income or cultural consonance could be masquerading, as it were, as the other variable by virtue of the fact that the two are correlated. One of these two variables could be a weak poseur, appearing to be important simply by riding on the coattails of the other variable.

This is why it is so important to be able to control or adjust for these patterns of correlations, to unpack these sorts of patterns. As Table 7.1 clearly shows, cultural consonance is the factor sharing variance with locus of control, and income is just along for the ride. Actually, the pattern of associations seen here is consistent with a causal sequence like this:

Income → Cultural Consonance → Locus of Control,

or, higher levels of income afford individuals the economic resources to achieve a lifestyle that is culturally valued, which in turn enhances their sense of personal agency.

The other thing to take away from Table 7.1 is a sense of how well this model fits the data, given by the **multiple R.** A simple bivariate correlation is denoted by a lowercase "r," whereas uppercase is used to denote a **multiple correlation coefficient.** In Model 3, age, sex, income, and cultural consonance combine to explain (in the statistical sense) 41% of the variance in locus of control. Is this good? Well, it looks pretty good to me, since we know that less than 100% of the variance is even explainable (owing to imperfections in measurement of the variables).

Someone might immediately object that I have no business making causal inferences with cross-sectional data (that is, data collected all in one fell swoop). This is a semireasonable objection in the sense that we don't really know what chicken or egg happened to come first here. However, I would argue that we are always in the business of making causal inferences, and cross-sectional data simply limit our confidence in the statements that we can make; I'm not saying that they outlaw certain kinds of statement. The main point here is that I've got a model, and I've got data consistent with that model. Granted, it is at one level a simple model—a straight line. But it's a real model and the data conform to it, and it rules out some alternative explanations, such as the oft-repeated critique that cultural consonance is just a proxy for socioeconomic status. If you don't like this model, let's first hear a reasoned, specific argument about it, and then let's see if you can do better. In the immortal words of Jerry Maguire: "Show me the money!"

This is just a bare taste of what you can do with multiple regression analysis. You could, for example, suggest that cultural consonance and locus of control have a curvilinear association (as I showed that cultural consonance and blood pressure have a curvilinear association) (Dressler 2005). Jim Bindon and I even had the temerity to suggest that, for people with one set of social relationships (social support from kin), cultural consonance and blood pressure would have a curvilinear association, whereas for people with another set of social relationships (social support from nonkin), cultural consonance and blood pressure would have a differently shaped relationship (Dressler and Bindon 2000). You might also think that increasing cultural consonance would not really decrease the likelihood of some outcome (like being depressed) until you achieved a certain level of cultural consonance and then—poof!—you would be launched into a different state (like not being depressed). In the biz this is what is called a **binary logistic regression** model. As I tell my students with respect to their hypotheses: if you can think it and you can say it, you can test it.

FACTOR ANALYSIS

Thus far we have focused our thinking in terms of dependent or outcome variables and of the independent variables we thought were antecedent or causal with respect to those outcomes. There are some research questions, however, that don't necessarily fit this causal thinking. For example, what if we think that there might be some kind of pattern in a set of data, but we don't necessarily know what that pattern is? There are various kinds of analyses that can be used to explore data for patterns that are not apparent to the eye, and some people refer to these as **techniques of numerical induction.** They include multidimensional scaling and cluster analysis, but the classic technique is certainly factor analysis.

Factor analysis as we know it has been around since the 1930s, but it became readily available to most researchers—for better or worse—only with access to digital computers in the late 1950s and early 1960s. To illustrate the use of factor analysis, I'm going to turn to a different sort of question and a different set of data. A venerable concern in anthropology has been sociocultural complexity. While foraging populations (or people subsisting by hunting and gathering) clearly possess a remarkably complex and subtle understanding of their environment and lively and complex belief systems, they also have a fairly limited material culture and relatively unelaborated social and political structure. Archaic states, in contrast, have complex material, social, and political structures, along with a nuanced understanding of their environment and elaborate belief systems. How can we usefully describe varying patterns of complexity of this sort among known societies in the world (Carneiro 1962)?

Factor analysis is a set of techniques that can be used to search patterns of correlations among variables. In this case, if we have a set of data on world societies that includes variables describing different societies' technologies, social structure, and political structure, we might examine the configuration of correlations to see if there is some pattern we might find interesting. The Human Relations Area Files (HRAF) and, more specifically, the Standard Ethnographic Sample (Murdock 1940) provide just such a set of data. The HRAF is a repository of ethnographic data on world societies, past and present, coded from ethnographies and related data sources. Once housed as slips of paper in row-on-row of filing cabinets, it is now online (http://hraf.yale.edu/). The Standard Ethnographic Sample is a sample of 186 societies drawn from the HRAF and related sources that have been shown to be relatively independent of one another; that is, the influence of diffusion from one society to another is relatively small. Hundreds of variables have been coded on these societies and various subsets of these societies (clearly not all ethnographers could report everything about the people among whom they worked, hence there are varying amounts of data on each society). There are obvious critiques of the whole enterprise of what is called cross-cultural survey research, such as the fact that when one is using these data it's impossible to study intracultural diversity since one is using a whole society as the unit of analysis. There are, however, some very interesting questions in anthropology and related social sciences that can be answered only by examining the most complete sample of human sociocultural variation, and the HRAF and the Standard Ethnographic Sample are it (see Ember & Ember 2009).

For this example, I have selected nine variables from the Standard Ethnographic Sample. These include: (1) monumental architecture, coded along an ordinal scale from the society not having any at all to one having large private and public buildings; (2) money, coded along an ordinal scale from not having a medium of exchange through various specialized kinds of media to having a true, generalized, abstract medium of value; (3) nonlocal political hierarchy, coded as the number of political administrative levels that exist beyond a local community; (4) local political hierarchy, coded as the number of political administrative levels within a local community; (5) population density, or the number of people per square mile in the community studied; (6) degree of social stratification, which is the number of social strata recognized; (7) land transport, coded as an ordinal scale from purely human power to wheeled vehicles; (8) writing and records, coded as an ordinal scale from no system of writing through to a true orthography and written records; and (9) degree of dependence on agriculture, expressed as a percentage of subsistence drawn from agriculture. (I'm just using the variables as they are coded in the data file; were this a true research effort, it would probably be a good idea to recode some of them.)

Factor analysis starts with a matrix of correlation coefficients, as shown in Table 7.2. The first thing notable about this correlation matrix is that it is a **full, square, symmetric matrix,** which means that it has the same number of rows as columns (which makes it square), and the upper half of the table is the same as the lower half (which makes it symmetric). The halves of the table are created by the diagonal, or the set of cells formed by the correlation of each variable with itself. Although at first glance the correlation of a variable with itself seems nonsensical, the diagonal of a correlation matrix can actually be quite useful and meaningful—but this is a topic beyond the level of the current discussion.

The next thing to notice is that the correlations between variables vary widely. For example, population density and reliance on agriculture are correlated at $r = .64$, whereas jurisdictional hierarchy at local and nonlocal levels are correlated at $r = .06$. Population density and agriculture tend to go together, while having more political hierarchy at the local level does not indicate greater hierarchy beyond the community, and vice versa. We could, of course, go through all 36 bivariate correlations in the table and try to figure out a pattern, and that is actually a very useful thing to do, always. However, having a model for discovering what patterns might exist in the table might be even more useful.

Factor analysis is often discussed in terms of **underlying dimensions** in the data. Right now there are nine dimensions in the matrix, because each variable can describe a part of the variation among societies on its own. But what if we could combine variables and argue that they go together to describe the data in a way that isn't obvious? We might even discover that there are underlying dimensions in the data. If the patterns of correlations among subsets of variables are high enough and patterned in a consistent way, then those variables might go together because they form part of one of these underlying dimensions.

These abstract notions are better discussed in the context of a concrete example. You can imagine what factor analysis is doing by envisioning it as a kind of thought experiment. What would happen if we thought of all

TABLE 7.2 Correlation matrix of social complexity variables from the Standard Cross-Cultural Sample

CORRELATION MATRIX

	Monumental architecture	Money	Nonlocal political hierarchy	Local political hierarchy	Population density	Degree of social stratification	Land transport	Writing & records	Dependence on agriculture
Monumental architecture	1.000	.367	.383	.077	.434	.383	.185	.377	.418
Money	.367	1.000	.559	.143	.582	.444	.419.	.531	.391
Nonlocal political hierarchy	.383	.559	1.000	.066	.547	.730	.518	.645	.538
Local political hierarchy	.077	.143	.066	1.000	.246	.087	-.028	.075	.276
Population density	.434	.582	.547	.246	1.000	.518	.215	.374	.643
Degree of social stratification	.383	.444	.730	.087	.518	1.000	.454	.602	.482
Land transport	.185	.419	.518	-.028	.215	.454	1.000	.628	.311
Writing and records	.377	.531	.645	.075	.374	.602	.628	1.000	.421
Dependence on agriculture	.418	.391	.538	.276	.643	.482	.311	.421	1.000

those nine variables as imperfect and observable manifestations of a single continuum along which societies can be ranked? If we knew how or had the technical capacity to measure that single continuum and locate each society along it, we would, but we can't. What we can do is measure what we know how to measure and try to zero in on that continuum. So we start by creating such a continuum—or dimension—taking into account the correlations among the variables. The idea here is that the variables that have the highest correlations with each other in Table 7.2, such as population density and dependence on agriculture, are so correlated because they each are highly correlated with this hypothetical continuum or dimension. From their observed correlation with each other, we can work backward and estimate what their correlation with this hypothetical dimension might be. Then, the variables that are most highly correlated with population density and dependence on agriculture, such as money and nonlocal political hierarchy, have those correlations because of their correlation with this hypothetical dimension. So we work backward from there to estimate what those correlations with this underlying dimension might be. And we keep doing this until the ability to estimate this first underlying dimension is exhausted.

In the process of analyzing the data in such a manner we are, in a sense, "explaining" the correlation between pairs of variables: they are correlated with each other because they both are correlated with this underlying dimension. But that correlation with the underlying dimension may not "explain" all of the correlation between two variables. There may be, in other words, some "residual" correlation that is not associated with that first dimension. A sufficiently large set of residual correlations suggests that there may be a second dimension. So, we proceed with our thought experiment, imagining what the correlations of all of the variables would look like with this dimension, if it existed.

And we continue with the analysis in this way until we have exhausted all the possible underlying dimensions. But of course, we want to be parsimonious. Things being equal, we prefer the simple model (Occam's razor). So we are trying to see if there is a simpler model that will describe the distribution of these societies.

It turns out that with these data, there is a two-dimensional model that fits the observations pretty well (and note that I am skipping over all sorts of technicalities here in terms of eigenvalues, communalities, decisions about the rank of the model, variance explained, factor rotation, and the different kinds of factor models—you can study up on these if you really want to use factor analysis). This model is shown in Table 7.3. The coefficients in this table can be interpreted as the correlation between a variable and the underlying dimension or factor. So, for the first factor, writing, land transportation, nonlocal political hierarchy, and degree of social stratification all have the highest correlation with this dimension. Money, dependence on agriculture, and population density are not unimportant, but they are less important than the other variables in uniquely identifying this dimension. For the second factor, population density, local political hierarchy, and dependence on agriculture are most important.

Are these meaningful patterns? What this analysis suggests is that these nine variables can be reduced to two factors that can be thought of as higher-order, or composite, variables. The first factor orders societies along a continuum defined in terms of social and technological complexity (money, transportation, writing, social stratification) and, especially, a political system that integrates communities beyond the local level. The second factor iden-

TABLE 7.3 Factor loadings for dimensions of sociocultural complexity

| | ROTATED COMPONENT MATRIX[a] | |
| | Component | |
	I	2
Writing and records	.833	.155
Land transport	.806	-.098
Nonlocal political hierarchy	.800	.328
Degree of social stratification	.740	.325
Money	.609	.411
Population density	.406	.742
Local political hierarchy	-.215	.712
Dependence on agriculture	.414	.691
Monumental agriculture	.383	.478

Extraction Method: Principal Component Analysis.
Rotation Method: Varimax with Kaiser Normalization.

[a] Rotation converged in 3 iterations.

tifies societies that are more densely populated and that have multiple administrative hierarchies in the local community but that involve little or no political integration beyond the local community. Presuming these are meaningful variables (and I hasten to add again that this is an example, not something I'm trying to defend), we would see that thinking about sociocultural complexity as a single dimension or continuum is incorrect. Sociocultural complexity comprises two dimensions.

The myriad ways that factor analysis has and can be applied would go well beyond the scope of this discussion. Suffice it to say that there are many (and we will explore one in the next section). There are other approaches that make different assumptions that can be used to explore the underlying structure of a set of data. **Nonmetric multidimensional scaling** can be a useful technique for visualizing patterns in certain kinds of data, especially because it does not assume that metric coefficients of similarity, such as the correlation coefficient, are being analyzed. Any kind of similarity or dissimilarity matrix can be analyzed. **Cluster analysis** and **correspondence analysis** are other models used to find structure in a set of data.

CULTURAL CONSENSUS ANALYSIS

Virtually every aspect of quantitative analysis we have discussed in this book applies to any type of investigation in which there is a sample of objects (respondents, plants, wolves, whatever) being examined in terms of a set of variables that might be associated in some way. The next technique I want to discuss briefly is different in the sense that it was developed to examine a specifically anthropological question: how is culture shared and distributed? **Cultural consensus analysis** (Romney, Weller, & Batchelder 1986) grew out of cognitive culture theory, in which culture is understood as that which one must know in order to function adequately in a given social system (Goodenough 1966). Culture is the knowledge and understanding, shared by individuals, used to make inferences about events and circumstances in the world, including the meaning of others' behavior, and to guide our own behavior. As a member of society, one learns this knowledge, and it is shared, because otherwise the relatively smooth operation of social interaction would be unlikely to occur. This knowledge is encoded in individual minds in the form of cultural models: skeletal, stripped-down representations of some cultural domain that include the elements of the domain and prototypical processes linking those elements. For example, the measure of cultural consonance in lifestyle that we have used in parts of this book is based on a cultural model of lifestyle in Brazil, in which individuals agree on the elements that make up a lifestyle and how those elements are ordered in importance for "having a life" (*para ter uma vida*) (see Dressler, Borges, Balieiro, & Dos Santos 2005; Dressler, Dos Santos, & Balieiro 1996 for an extended discussion). This cultural model orders people's thinking and behavior in this domain.

The problem in anthropology for the last 125 years or so is that sharing has been assumed rather than demonstrated. The degree to which understanding in a domain is shared, or the degree to which it is not shared or even contested, has not been made problematic and subject to empirical investigation. Yet, it is a central question in anthropology. Because the cultural consensus model enables us to tackle this question in a way that is both theoretically and methodologically satisfying, I regard it as a real paradigm changer (see Dressler, Balieiro, & Dos Santos 2015).

The cultural consensus model (CCM), or **cultural consensus analysis** (CCA)—I use the two interchangeably—works from the agreement among respondents regarding knowledge in or the understanding of some cultural domain. There are different ways that this agreement can be assessed, depending on how a question is asked. For example, you might give people a list of statements or propositions that they can either agree or disagree with. These would be dichotomous responses. The degree to which two people agree in their responses can then be assessed as, basically, the proportion of statements on which they give the same answer. This is a kind of **simple matching coefficient.**

If people have been asked to rank or rate something, a correlation coefficient can be used to assess similarities in responses. For example, in the case of the elements of lifestyle in Brazil, people were asked to rank the items from most to least important. These rankings for different individuals can then be correlated.

There are two forms of the cultural consensus model that can be applied to these data (see Weller 2007 for a thorough discussion of CCA). One form is a fully axiomatic, logico-deductive model. According to this model, if we make a few assumptions, we can use a set of mathematical axioms to deduce the solution to the question of how we can tell if a group of people agree on something. An important assumption that must be made in applying this **formal process model** involves the nature of the data: the model applies only to questions to which the answer is a dichotomy (yes-no, true-false, agree-disagree).

The second form of the model is called the **informal data model,** and it applies to data that take the form of ranks or ratings (for example, on a 4-point scale from strongly disagree to strongly agree). It is informal because the mathematical elegance is not there. In practice it will give you nearly the same results as the formal model, but you can't derive all of the steps mathematically. I tend to use the informal data model because I have found, in practice, that people tend not to think about things in quite the definite terms implied by the stark choice between "true" and "false." My experience, in societies ranging from peasant communities in central Mexico to urban Brazil, is that people like to have a little wiggle room. Maybe they are not definitely sure that something such as owning a cell phone is important for having a good life, but they might think that it is at least somewhat important.

I now present an extended example of cultural consensus analysis, embedded in a larger cultural domain analysis. As discussed by Borgatti (1994, 1999), cultural domain analysis includes an extensive set of techniques, the aim of which is to facilitate eliciting the categories and criteria that people use every day in meaningfully organizing the world around them.

I argue in the next chapter that a large part of our job as ethnographers is to discover how people cognitively organize their worlds. One of the steps in this analysis, after we come up with some hypotheses about the criteria or principles that people are using in thinking about the world, is to determine if people *share* with each other this understanding or knowledge of the world: is it, in short, a *cultural* understanding of the world? What follows is an extended example of a cultural domain analysis, in a familiar cultural domain—music—that illustrates this approach. Most important, it illustrates the application of the correlation coefficient in new and interesting ways, from examining the similarities and differences in the understanding of musical styles among a group of college students to determining just how much these students are using this shared understanding to solve a real-world problem. In this case, the problem will be a question about how they would group these musical styles. The analytic technique that enables us to examine this question is the correlation coefficient.

To do cultural consensus analysis, you have a set of questions that apply to a cultural domain, and you ask a sample of (at least 30) people to respond to these questions. One year, when teaching these methods in a class on cognitive anthropology, I elicited from students a list of terms/phrases describing the cultural domain "music that people listen to around here." The list included the following terms:

Gospel	Christian
Rock	Alternative
Metal	Jam
Punk	Indie
Pop	Oldies
Techno	Disco
Funk	R&B
Soul	Rap
Hip-hop	Zydeco
Cajun	Reggae
World music	Celtic
Salsa	Country
Bluegrass	Folk
Classical	Opera
Jazz	Blues

Next, to elicit the criteria that people use to distinguish one kind of music from another, the students did an **unconstrained pile sort.** Each music term was written on a card, and each student sorted the 30 terms into piles. They could make as many, or as few, piles as they wished (hence it was "unconstrained"), with the only stipulations being that they should put musical genres into groups based on their similarities and they should create as many groups as they needed in order to have similar styles within each group. With those data you can create a full, square, symmetric matrix of musical terms. The similarity of each pair of terms can be assessed by the percentage of students who place two terms in the same pile. Then, I analyzed that matrix of similarities using nonmetric multidimensional scaling, a technique mentioned in the last section. The point of this technique is to see if we can represent, or visualize, these similarities in a reduced set of dimensions—two would be nice, so that we can look at a picture on a page (a piece of paper has two dimensions: height and width). With multidimensional scaling we can try out a two-dimensional representation of similarities and differences among musical styles and then check to see if that model corresponds closely to the original data. If it does, then we can use it as a literal, visual model of how the musical genres are distributed relative to each other.

The pile sort data using these musical terms fit quite nicely into two dimensions, and that picture is reproduced as Figure 7.1. In addition to multidimensional scaling, I have also cluster-analyzed the similarities and differences among the musical styles, which enables me to draw circles around the genres that end up in the same grouping. Multidimensional scaling is good for representing the distances among a set of elements; cluster analysis is good for finding boundaries among groups.

As you can see, gospel and Christian music are up in the northwest corner of the graph, whereas all the world music genres are opposite them in the southeast corner. Due north of the world music genres and due east of gospel are opera and classical music, with bluegrass hanging out quite close by. You can see clearly how other genres relate, because the graph provides a kind of cognitive map of music.

FIGURE 7.1 Multidimensional scaling of a pile sort of musical genres

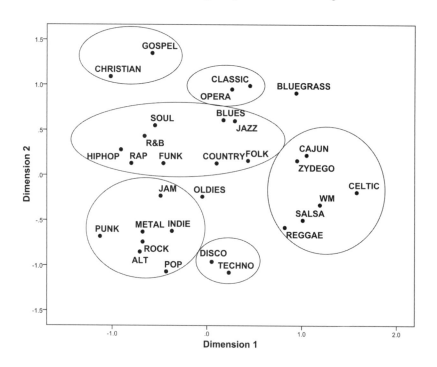

The question becomes: what criteria or features of music were people attending to when they did the pile sort? In plain language, what were people thinking? And, the anthropological question is: were they, more or less, thinking about the same things, thus indicating an underlying cultural model for the domain "music people listen to around here?" We get at these criteria or features through open-ended interviewing during and after the pile sort, which in the context of these data was a class discussion. There are quite a few criteria that people mentioned, including the historic origins of the music, whether or not you can dance to it (which I think of as the "American Bandstand" feature—and if you don't know what I mean, google "American Bandstand" and learn a little about the pop culture history of the mid- to late 20th century). But students seemed that year (and in previous years) to fasten on a feature that they had a surprisingly hard time articulating. Sometimes students referred to this feature as "complexity," which seems to indicate literally the number of notes in the music and also the technical skill required to play it (why else would bluegrass end up near to classical music?). In this particular class, however, students talked more in terms of the music being "popular" music versus a more esoteric, "specialized" kind of art form.

To determine if people are using any or all of these features in thinking about music, you have to collect more data. So, I had the class rate each musical style on a 4-point scale indicating the degree to which the style conformed to that feature. They thus rated each musical style on the degree to which the style was popular or was a specialized art form. The first step in analyzing these data was to determine if the students agreed with one another on the rating of musical styles; hence I used cultural consensus analysis.

CCA can be a little confusing at the outset, because we are shifting our thinking by 90°. What I mean is that so far we have been analyzing variables as characterizing respondents and, for example, seeing if cultural consonance is associated with locus of control. Here the point is to evaluate cultural consensus or sharing, so we want to see if respondents are related to one another. To do this we correlate respondents in terms of their profiles of answers to questions. A correlation matrix of 10 students who completed this task is shown in Table 7.4. Keep in mind that what we have done here is to arrange the data so that each student can be compared with every other student in terms of how they rated each musical style. We are literally correlating people across the information, rather than correlating information (or variables) across people.

TABLE 7.4 Correlations among students in their ratings of musical genres as "popular" versus "specialized" art forms

		1	2	3	4	5	6	7	8	9	10
1	Michelle	1.00	0.28	0.21	0.32	0.46	0.40	0.26	0.56	0.50	0.14
2	Becky	0.28	1.00	0.20	0.68	0.79	0.69	0.77	0.46	0.70	0.49
3	Catherine	0.21	0.20	1.00	0.37	0.22	0.23	0.22	0.47	0.35	0.37
4	Stone	0.32	0.68	0.37	1.00	0.66	0.73	0.70	0.57	0.64	0.77
5	Stephanie	0.46	0.79	0.22	0.66	1.00	0.75	0.79	0.62	0.76	0.45
6	Lena	0.40	0.69	0.23	0.73	0.75	1.00	0.70	0.70	0.70	0.56
7	Sarah	0.26	0.77	0.22	0.70	0.79	0.70	1.00	0.42	0.64	0.54
8	Curry	0.56	0.46	0.47	0.57	0.62	0.70	0.42	1.00	0.72	0.46
9	Shaundra	0.50	0.70	0.35	0.64	0.76	0.70	0.64	0.72	1.00	0.48
10	Evan	0.14	0.49	0.37	0.77	0.45	0.56	0.54	0.46	0.48	1.00

Looking at the first column we see that Michelle is not really answering questions regarding the "artiness" of the music very much, as the other students are. Looking at the next column for Becky, we see that, except for her low agreement with Michelle and Catherine, she agrees quite a bit with other students. The strongest pattern of correlations is for Stephanie who, with again the exception of a couple students, agrees strongly with other students.

What CCA does, in overly simple terms, is a factor analysis of people, working from this correlation matrix. Remember in the last section that we said that factor analysis is searching for an underlying dimension? Can we imagine an unobserved underlying dimension in which our observed individual people are imperfect manifestations? That underlying factor would be the shared cultural model of musical genres. Each individual has his or her own variant of that model, and in one sense it is an imperfect reproduction of the shared cultural model.

The CCA of these data is shown in Table 7.5. The first thing to look at here is the part of the table labeled "estimated knowledge of each respondent." This part comprises the correlations of each respondent with the underlying cultural model (and are factor loadings, as we discussed in the previous section). Is there a shared cultural model? One answer to that

TABLE 7.5 Cultural consensus analysis of the ratings of musical genres as "popular" versus "specialized" art forms

CONSENSUS ANALYSIS				
EIGENVALUES				
Factor	Value	Percent	Cum %	Ratio
-------	-------	-------	-------	-------
1:	5.526	79.9	79.9	7.353
2:	0.751	10.9	90.8	1.181
3:	0.636	9.2	100.0	
=======	=======	=======	=======	=======
	6.913	100.0		

Estimated Knowledge of each Respondent

1	Michelle	0.46
2	Becky	0.80
3	Catherine	0.38
4	Stone	0.84
5	Stephanie	0.87
6	Lena	0.86
7	Sarah	0.80
8	Curry	0.74
9	Shaundra	0.85
10	Evan	0.65

Average: 0.724
Std. Dev.: 0.167

question involves the size and standard deviation of the mean knowledge estimates, referred to as **cultural competence** in CCA. Here it is .724 (± .167). This is a fairly high mean correlation, indicating a shared cultural model or way of thinking about music. For a second answer to that question look at the top of the table and the ratio of the 1st to the 2nd eigenvalue. I avoided talking about eigenvalues in the previous section on factor analysis, but I can't avoid it now. Remember that the first factor tries to account for all of the highest correlations among, in the case, people. This is the same thing as saying that the first factor should explain as much of the variance as possible—it should provide a dimension that explains why all those people have high correlations between them (and remember that the answer in the factor model is because they are all highly correlated with the underlying dimension, in this case the cultural model). Well, one interpretation of an eigenvalue is that it summarizes the variance explained by the factor, or in this case how well the factor explains correlations among individuals. But of course, it won't—it can't—explain all of the variation, so factor analysis then looks for a second factor to explain additional variance, and CCA does the same thing. The logic of CCA is that if the first factor explains a substantially greater amount of the variance than the second factor does—traditionally about three times as much—then you can reasonably make the inference that there is a shared cultural model operating here.

In the case of music, that ratio is 7.35:1, which, along with the high mean cultural competence, increases our confidence that everybody is on the same page in their thinking, and that page is a shared cultural model. Finally, looking at the distribution of cultural competence, we see that everybody tends to have high, positive coefficients. The exceptions, as we could have guessed from the correlation matrix, are Michelle and Catherine. Their ratings of the music tended to indicate more of their own idiosyncratic thought than what they shared with other people.

The final thing we can do with CCA is to estimate the ratings of the music based on the collective, consensus model. We have the ratings of each of the 10 students. We also have their cultural competence, or how well they reproduce the hypothetical, underlying dimension that is the cultural model. Well, that cultural model is specifically the group-level ratings of the music, which we can estimate from an average of the 10 students' ratings, *except that* we don't use a simple average. Rather, we give greater weight to the students with higher cultural competence. So, in calculating these ratings, what Stephanie thinks counts more than what Catherine thinks. In this sense, these estimated ratings of the music represent the cultural model, not some simple average, and they are a **cultural best estimate** of the ratings of the music. If we invited another student to rate the music, and we thought that this student would be reasonably culturally competent, then these ratings are what we would expect that student to, more-or-less, reproduce.

There's one more step we can take here to examine how well these data all fit together. The configuration of musical styles represented visually in Figure 7.1 is a result of the students' using all their cultural knowledge to organize the genres. If that is true, then the consensus ratings of the music in terms of "artiness" ought to be associated with the way in which the genres have been sorted (and, of course, there should be other criteria related to that as well, but we'll just look at "artiness"). The distance between pairs of musical genres in Figure 7.1 should be associated with the differing ratings of the music on "artiness." To evaluate this anticipated correlation, we can again employ multiple regression analysis, but in a different way. Here, we can use the cultural consensus ratings of "artiness" as a dependent variable and the coordinates that locate the musical genres in cultural space as the independent variables. In this analysis, the musical genres themselves become the units of analysis, and the ways in which they vary—the variables—are

FIGURE 7.2 Multidimensional scaling of pile sort of musical genres with cultural consensus ratings of "popular" versus "specialized" art forms plotted as a regression line

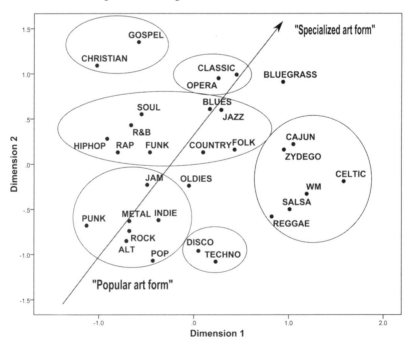

the multidimensional scaling coordinates from the pile sorts and the cultural consensus ratings from the cultural consensus analysis.

When we do this, there is a multiple correlation coefficient of $R = .86$ ($p < .001$) between the coordinates and the cultural consensus ratings. And we can draw that straight line in the graph, to produce Figure 7.2. So indeed, it appears as though the collective configuration of musical genres is a result, in part, of a shared notion of "popular" versus "art" styles of music. Some readers may recoil at the notion that bluegrass music ends up so close in this graphic to opera and classical music. I would point out two things, however. First, it doesn't actually end up in the same cluster as opera and classical, just in the same vicinity. It is located there as much by what it is not close to (and hence not sorted with) as by what it is sorted with. Second, I am reminded of the story of one of Mozart's patrons supposedly exclaiming, on hearing a new composition: "Very pretty my dear Mozart, but so many notes!" Next time you hear a David Grisman or Chris Thile mandolin riff, think about the technical competence and virtuosity required.

SUMMARY

My aim in this chapter has been to provide at least a taste of the gravy that comes with absorbing the 5 things you need to know about statistics. The examples given in this chapter are all based on the idea of the correlation coefficient and the ways in which the properties of the correlation coefficient can be exploited so that we can understand basic anthropological questions. The questions that have been addressed range from medical and psychological anthropology (that is, what factors influence locus of control?); to general cultural evolutionary theory (what is the nature of sociocultural complexity?); and to cognitive anthropology (is there a cultural model of musical styles among U.S. undergraduates?). Numeric analyses enabled us to look at each of these questions in a nuanced way, and a way that leads to new discoveries and new directions in research. With respect to locus of control, it would appear that a cultural process—cultural consonance—mediates the expression of this psychological disposition. With respect to sociocultural complexity, a single dimension of complexity appears to be inadequate to account for cross-cultural variability. With respect to musical genres, students appear to employ a multifaceted and shared model in thinking about these styles. By employing numeric analysis, new insights are gained.

Again, this chapter gave you just a taste of the ways in which a basic statistical model—the correlation coefficient—can be adapted to address different questions. I strongly recommend that you consult Bernard (2011) and Handwerker and Borgatti (2014) for more examples.

Integrating Quantitative Research in Anthropological Research Design

At this point, I want to turn to some broader issues of anthropological research—especially how the collection of numeric data can be integrated into ethnographic research. Mixed-methods research has become a kind of default mode for people with a scientific orientation in anthropology, which is good, but there are nagging questions of both logic and practice in actually doing mixed-methods research. In this chapter, I address some of these issues.

WHAT'S THE POINT OF ANTHROPOLOGICAL RESEARCH?

Certainly, one answer to this question is that the point of anthropological research is to document and to try to understand human behavior, social organization, and culture in all of its many manifestations. This is the broadest intellectual point of it all. More prosaically, however, this is a question that is often posed in less intellectual tones by university administrators who are deciding whether to continue funding for a department or a particular faculty position, and by those who control other sorts of purse strings. As I write this yet another member of the U.S. Congress has proposed that funding for social scientific research be drastically cut at the National Science Foundation, and anthropologists often find themselves uncomfortably in the cross-hairs of such targeted cuts, because our research can be easy to mock, however spurious that mockery might be. So, what's the real point of what we do? Don't other social scientists do all that needs to be done, and better, while they crunch away at their huge data sets?

Anthropologists have grappled with this question off and on for a long time. For example, I have always suspected that Alfred Kroeber (1917)

The 5 Things You Need to Know about Statistics: Quantification in Ethnographic Research by William W. Dressler, 133–147 © 2015 Left Coast Press, Inc. All rights reserved.

resurrected Spencer's idea of the "superorganic" in part as a way of justifying the creation of a nearly new field of study, with the attendant needs for brick-and-mortar departments, museums, and so on. After all, if he could argue for what is, in essence, another order of reality, then there needed to be somebody around to study it, and we are that somebody.

I think that a major aim of anthropology—not the only point, but a major point nonetheless—was actually being invented at the same time that Kroeber was writing, but half-way around the world in a Trobriand village. I of course am referring to Malinowski and his "invention" of ethnographic fieldwork. Boas and his followers had been going about collecting primary data for some time, although they could be surprisingly unsystematic in the data they collected, and they did not seem overly concerned about doing what a friend of mine terms "drive-by ethnography" (swooping into a community, grabbing some data, and swooping back out). It was Malinowski who, despite all his faults and failings, argued that settling into residence in a community and learning and living in the local language were essential in anthropological fieldwork and were in the service of the primary aim of ethnography. "This goal is, briefly, to grasp the native's point of view, his relation to life, to realize *his* vision of *his* world" (Malinowski 1961 [original 1922]: 24; emphasis in the original).

Fast-forward 32 years and Kenneth Pike (1954) formalizes the emic-etic distinction in anthropology. From an **etic perspective** we describe and analyze human behavior solely in terms that have been developed by the investigator or, more accurately, in the theoretical systems that investigator employs to derive his or her research questions and hypotheses. So, if we go into a community to study the psychological disposition of locus of control, it does not make any difference at all whether this notion of individual agency (or lack thereof) is something that the community's people think about. If theoreticians of repute have deemed that it is important in explaining human behavior, then it is.

From an **emic perspective,** in contrast, we describe and analyze human behavior in terms that are meaningful to the participants. In this approach we first determine what sorts of broad domains of life are important to people, based on the fact that they talk about those domains. We then try to understand how those domains are semantically structured and, ultimately, to determine the extent of sharing of the knowledge underlying that structure and how that shared knowledge—or cultural model—is distributed (see the example of musical genres in the preceding chapter). And there are other approaches to the study of communities from an emic perspective, including especially interpretive analyses.

I would not say that an emic perspective is totally missing from other social scientific fields (for example, consider phenomenological sociology). More often this perspective tends to get smuggled in and not explicitly acknowledged. But I would argue that an emic perspective, or what could also be termed a cultural constructivist orientation, has been elevated to a more intense intellectual and theoretical focus in anthropology than in any other field.

In part this intellectual focus grew out of the process of doing traditional fieldwork. However, I emphatically do not want to imply that anthropology as a field is defined by ethnographic fieldwork or, even worse, qualitative methods. There are a couple of problems with such a definition. One is purely intellectual. A field of inquiry cannot logically be defined by its methods. What defines a field of inquiry is its focus of study and the questions it poses. Any field of study confronts a world that is regarded as structured and differentiated, and it seeks to uncover the underlying processes that operate in that world. For anthropology, this process is all about the astounding variation in human behavior, social organization, and culture that exists around the globe and through time. How do we describe that? How did it come to be? How is it maintained and changed? And, anthropology, as I have argued, takes seriously the idea that the ways in which people understand the world around them is an important component in accounting for behavior, social organization, and culture.

There are also practical reasons why defining a field of study in terms of its methods is problematic. I'm not sure how it works in other topical areas of study, but there is a depressingly familiar scenario that occurs in medical anthropology. Medical anthropology is, of course, devoted to the study of culture, health, and healing. As such, it interfaces with other fields that study health and healing, especially in the public health sciences. Inevitably, discussions arise regarding how medical anthropology intersects with epidemiology, the hyper-quantitative public health science. If epidemiology is not the poster child for big-time number crunching, I don't know what is. When the discussion of anthropology and epidemiology surfaces at an anthropology meeting, for example, inevitably somebody gets up and says that we can apply qualitative methods to epidemiology. The problem is that this particular train left the station a long time ago. There are some exceptionally good and thoughtful guides to qualitative methods by anthropologists (such as Bernard & Ryan [2010] and DeWalt & DeWalt [2011]); however, formalizing qualitative methods has been a cottage industry for 30 years in education, nursing, and sociology, to name but a few fields. Any public health scientists who want to learn and/or apply qualitative methods in their research need not turn to anthropology or seek out an anthropologist as a collaborator.

So, for both logical and practical reasons, anthropology should not be defined by its methods. Rather, anthropology should be defined by its interest in cross-cultural comparison and by its interest in incorporating emic terms into its theories and explanations. This perspective is what makes it relatively unique among the social sciences, and the implications of this idea for mixed-methods research in anthropology are explored next.

MIXED-METHODS RESEARCH IN ANTHROPOLOGY

The gold standard in anthropological research remains the prototype defined by Malinowski: long-term residence in a community, learning and working in a local language, and trying to understand the world as it is culturally constructed by the members of that community. I would add to this approach testing hypotheses and research questions that are theoretically important and especially seeing how emic terms enter into the processes described by the theory.

The process begins ultimately with theory and a question. For example, in my dissertation research in the late 1970s, I went into the field with a question regarding the risk of cardiovascular disease in a modernizing society (St. Lucia in the eastern Caribbean). Lots of descriptive data from many parts of the world showed that, over time, as societies were increasingly exposed to modernizing influences, the risk of cardiovascular disease increased. This fact could be conveniently measured by blood pressure (Henry & Cassel 1969)—high blood pressure is a health problem in its own right and a major precursor of other cardiovascular diseases. One argument was that this kind of social change (modernization) was stressful, which led me to explore what came to be known as the stress model of disease (Lazarus 1966). Briefly, the stress model posits two kinds of psychosocial influences on the risk of disease. The first consists of stressors, or events and circumstances, that demand some kind of adjustive response from an individual, hence taxing his or her psychological, social, and physical resources. The second consists of resources for resisting or adjusting to stressors, including especially the kinds of social support from others that an individual can access.

Before going into the field, and throughout my year-long fieldwork, my job in part was to engage in what I later termed "the ethnographic critique of theory" (Dressler 1995). There are lots of interesting theories of human behavior, and few of them have been subjected to intense and detailed cross-cultural scrutiny. Therefore, a major anthropological question is: how do the terms and proposed processes in a theory translate into reality on the ground in a very different setting?

Take for example the term *social support*. Theoretically, it encompasses both seeking emotional support and information from others, as well as seeking concrete material resources from others. In a social system guided by voluntarism in social relationships like ours (that is, we can voluntarily enter into social relationships with pretty much anyone we care to), systems of social support have been thought of as pretty flexible and up to the individual. I once heard Lisa Berkman, one of the foremost epidemiological researchers on social support (Berkman & Kawachi 2000), confidently assert that it did not matter at all who provided social support. As long as it was available, that was all that mattered with respect to stress and coping.

The local setting of St. Lucia provides an interesting twist on this. Members of the rural proletariat in the West Indies turn out to be fairly skeptical regarding others' trustworthiness and motives in social interaction. This skepticism leads them to rely heavily on kin for social support, and in the middle-aged sample that I focused on, adult siblings were particularly important. Also, patterns of family and household formation lead to complex networks of households with reciprocal rights and obligations. As described by the great ethnographer of the West Indies, M. G. Smith (1962), formal marriage, establishing an independent household, and having children are not linked in a temporal sequence as they are (or, at least, as they once were) in middle-class strata in Europe and North America. The majority of St. Lucians in my research had children with one or more other people before settling down to a conjugal household consisting of a man and woman, their children in common, and the woman's children from previous relationships. Marriage then followed the establishment of this household. This also meant that the man had "outside" children in other households. This was a well-described pattern and had usually been labeled as an example of "social disorganization" by North American social scientists (Smith 1971). But was it really indicative of social disorganization?

It had been suggested by some that this pattern of family and household formation was in fact quite the opposite of social disorganization—that it could instead be viewed as an adaptation to the extreme economic marginality endured by the West Indian rural proletariat. In my fieldwork, one of the first things I learned was that the highest form of moral failure a man could experience was to deny paternity. A true man must not only recognize and acknowledge his children, he must also provide them with support. This could range from as small a contribution as buying their pencils for the new school year to giving them cash regularly. The point is that there is a network of households linked by children through which resources flow. This situation also provides aging parents with a broader system of potential support when they no longer can support themselves.

So, far from social disorganization, this arrangement began to look like a support system, although one quite different from that envisioned by North American epidemiologists. And, having such a network of support was associated with lower blood pressure. Furthermore, the combination of this and other kin-based support was an effective buffer against the stresses generated by, and experienced as, a part of the modernization process (Dressler 1979, 1982).

The point here is that an emic understanding of family and household formation was necessary to understand how these factors influenced stress and the risk of disease. Could a social scientist have dreamed this up without doing ethnographic fieldwork? Perhaps. But ethnographic fieldwork is the best way of carrying out this kind of systematic discovery procedure. In a conventional philosophy of social science, scientific activity is divided into processes of **discovery** and **verification** (Rudner 1966). Discovery refers literally to the generation of hypotheses, and there is thought not to be a logic of discovery. Hypotheses are, rather, bold predictions about the world that can come from anywhere. There is a logic to verification, or rather more accurately hypothesis testing, that lays out how we can come to have more or less confidence in what we say about the world, and this process has been the major focus of this book.

Ethnography, I think, alters the division of labor between discovery and verification and instead links them in a logical way. Yes, research questions and hypotheses are generated by our intuition and theoretical acumen, but the ethnographic critique of theory, or seeing how the key terms in our questions get transformed on the ground in real communities and among people interacting, provides us with a kind of logic of discovery. Ultimately, we can use this approach to incorporate terms with high **emic validity** into our explanatory models and compare and contrast the predictive efficacy of those terms against other kinds of factors.

I return to this point in a moment, but right now I want to consider an oft-repeated critique of the incorporation of quantitative data into anthropological research design, best illustrated by a story. When I was finishing my dissertation, I went on an interview for a job in a medical school. After my job talk, an epidemiologist (who, later on, turned out to be a good friend and great supporter of my work) simply asserted that my statistical results were no good because my sample size was too small. In my fieldwork I spent the first eight months of my stay engaged in traditional participant-observation and key-informant interviewing, as well as carrying out a small side-study with a sample of patients in treatment for high blood pressure (see Dressler 1980). For my main survey to test hypotheses regarding social and cultural factors associated with blood pressure I interviewed 100 people, aged 40–49. As I noted earlier, I focused exclusively on this age group because in descriptive epidemiology this is the group within which blood pressure tends to vary the most, probably because life-long experience, including the experiences of family formation, is catching up with people and having its effects. Therefore it seemed like a good, targeted sample for detecting the effects in which I was interested. Why a sample of 100? It seemed like a large enough sample to observe statistical effects, and, as important, it seemed like a sample that I could actually interview (with the help of my research assistant) in the three months I had budgeted for this phase of the research.

I discussed earlier the importance of sample size with respect to statistical power, or the ability to detect a statistical association if in fact there is one. And, of course, sampling is essential to obtaining a valid representation of the population one is dealing with. In presentations of statistics the discussion of sampling can get complicated, but nevertheless one comes away with the impression that size matters—the bigger the sample size, the better. (I recently went through this with a research grant proposal to the National Institutes of Health. The critique of too-small sample size comes to feel like a mantra.)

In my job interview I stumbled through an inadequate response (it was early in my career, after all). What I should have pointed out was that my critic would have been absolutely correct *if* I had been doing conventional epidemiology or sociology. But I was not. The findings from the quantitative phase of my research were not stand-alone findings (as they would have been in a purely quantitative field); rather, these findings were embedded in ethnography and could not, nor should not, be considered apart from the converging evidence drawn from all the ethnographic research. My results were, to a certain extent, counterintuitive, and their interpretation depended on the ethnographic data demonstrating that St. Lucians thought about their children and their families in ways different from North American social and public health scientists. My results depended, in short, on that emic perspective. This simple fact sets ethnographic results from quantitative research apart from results from a purely statistical survey. The strength of the evidence stems from the convergence of ethnographic and quantitative methods.

A few years later I was discussing these and related results in another setting. In that presentation I emphasized the dislocating effects of social change and modernization in communities both inside and outside the industrialized north. In my early fieldwork I suggested that these dislocating effects led to a changing emphasis in systems of social status and that for many individuals achieving a modicum (not a maximum) of status was, at least, complicated, which in turn resulted in a stressful incongruence in status for them. This, prolonged over years, in turn was associated with higher blood pressure (Dressler 1985). Another epidemiologist friend pointed out that I really could not talk about these effects as being the result of social change and modernization, because I did not have longitudinal data (data collected at two or more points in time). I again stumbled over my response, but I realize now that it wasn't a matter of not having the data, it was a matter of how wide the confidence intervals are that you can put around your statements. My results were based, in part, on ethnographic and historical data laying out a particular narrative trajectory for a community relative to social organization and especially social status. This narrative trajectory resulted in the hypothesis that status incongruence (of a particular kind, measured in an emically valid way) would be associated with higher blood pressure. And, this hypothesis was confirmed.

Would it have been better to have longitudinal, quantitative data? Of course, but this would have truly required at least repeated cross-sectional, if not true prospective, samples for each decade starting in the 1940s (see Dressler and Oths (2014) for a discussion of the distinction between cross-sectional and prospective data). That is a bit pie-in-the-sky, I think. Rather, the converging trends of ethnographic and historical evidence lead to the anticipation of an association between two specific variables (controlling, of course, for known covariates and competing explanatory factors). If the anticipated statistical association is observed, then it lends credence and confidence to the entire explanatory narrative.

Confidence in that narrative is also bolstered by replication. Through a happy coincidence, I had the good fortune to replicate my results from St. Lucia in Mexico (Dressler, Mata, Chavez, & Viteri 1987), Brazil (Dressler, Dos Santos, Gallagher, & Viteri 1987), Jamaica (Dressler, Grell, & Viteri 1995), and the African American community in the southern United States (Dressler 1990) over a period of about 10 years. Although my own personal ethnographic work was extensive only in Brazil and the southern United States, immersion in the existing ethnographic literature and brief field trips proved to be invaluable for the other research sites and provided enough context and background for the development of emically valid measures. The overall results were replicated, although measurements were specifically tailored to each setting. These replications led to my later arguments that the stressors generated by the modernization process were generally quite similar across settings but that the social resources for adjusting to those stressors varied substantially in terms of local social organization (Dressler 1994, 1995).

My main point here is, again, that as anthropologists and ethnographers we are not doing the same thing with our quantitative methods as our brothers and sisters in more heavily quantitatively oriented disciplines. Our quantitative methods come bundled in a larger ethnographic enterprise.

EMIC VALIDITY

As Malinowski pointed out a century ago, the aim of this ethnographic enterprise is to understand and represent the world as others see it, as best we can. At the same time, it is problematic to adopt a strong (in the philosophical sense of that term) cultural constructivist orientation. My thinking in this regard has been influenced by the earlier writings of Pierre Bourdieu (1984). Bourdieu recommended what I and others have referred to as a "structural-constructivist" perspective (Dressler 2001, 2007b; Dressler, Oths, & Gravlee 2005). Boiled down to its basics, a structural-constructivist perspective orients us to consider how people make the world around them meaningful in singular ways and behave in terms of that meaning; and, at the same time, this perspective demands that we must take into account how the world is structured and differentiated in ways outside that shared understanding. Therefore, at times, cultural construction and structural constraint collide. However the emic and etic interact, both must be taken into account.

What this means is that in our research designs, we either discover emic constructs that shape lived experience for people, or we discover how key theoretical constructs get emically transformed by local systems of shared meaning. We then systematically develop measurements of those constructs that can be incorporated into multivariate statistical models. The way in which shared meaning modifies social processes at the local level—captured by our emic measures and the ways in which we specify our statistical models—can then be compared to and contrasted with purely etic theoretical constructs.

What we seek, then, are measurements with emic validity. In formal terms, an emically valid measurement is one that orders people along a continuum defined in terms that those people use to talk about that particular cultural domain. It locates people in a space of shared meaning. This is what I was doing with my measure of social support in St. Lucia. Through key-informant interviewing and participant-observation, I developed a way to gather data in order to tabulate and code the number of outside children that people had, that in turn served as an indicator of their integration into a network of resources. Janes (1990) and Oths, Dunn, and Palmer (2001) provide excellent examples of using traditional ethnographic techniques in the development of emically valid measurements.

In the past few years I have been working on a set of techniques for the development of emically valid measures in my work on cultural consonance (Dressler, Borges, Balieiro, & Dos Santos 2005; Dressler, Dos Santos, & Balieiro 1996). As noted earlier, cultural consonance is the degree to which individuals approximate, in their own beliefs and behaviors, prototypes for belief and behavior encoded in shared cultural models. This construct refers then to the extent to which individuals actually incorporate these shared ideas into their lives. The measure of cultural consonance in lifestyle that we used in Chapters 5 and 7 was actually my first attempt at creating an emically valid measure of cultural consonance in a specific cultural domain (Dressler 1996; Dressler, Dos Santos, & Balieiro 1996). In that research we developed an inventory of lifestyle items through key-informant interviewing and participant-observation and then verified that there was a shared understanding regarding a "good" or "valued" lifestyle using cultural consensus analysis. This generated an inventory of more-or-less valued lifestyle items. The measure of cultural consonance in lifestyle is then simply the proportion of the highly valued lifestyle items that people own (or activities they participate in).

In more recent studies (Dressler, Balieiro, & Dos Santos 2015; Dressler, Balieiro, Ribeiro, & Dos Santos 2005) we have refined this approach to measurement by using all the techniques of cultural domain analysis (Borgatti 1994, 1999; Weller & Romney 1988). The advantage to the techniques of cultural domain analysis is that they help to remove more of the judgment and inconsistencies of the interviewer from the elicitation of terms that structure and organize a cultural domain. The approach of cultural domain analysis was discussed in Chapter 7 in conjunction with the example of the domain of musical genres. Briefly (and see the papers cited in this chapter for more detail), these techniques begin with free-listing to elicit terms that structure a cultural domain. Once an adequate list of terms (or phrases, depending on the domain) has been elicited, a sampling of these elements can be selected to represent the cultural domain and used for further study. One very useful technique to be used with these terms is pile sorting. Through pile sorting you can develop hypotheses about the dimensions of meaning that people use in thinking about the domain (for example, "artiness" in the musical genre domain). The process then culminates in the collection of data to verify whether or not people share an understanding of that domain, using cultural consensus analysis.

Remember that the cultural answer key from cultural consensus analysis provides a cultural best estimate of the responses to questions phrased about a particular cultural domain. These responses can then be used to develop questions for individuals and their own beliefs and behaviors, to determine how closely they approximate that cultural prototype. In the case of cultural consonance in lifestyle, from cultural consensus analysis we obtained the rank, from most important to least important, of lifestyle items and behaviors that contribute having a good life (although, unironically, our informants insisted on just saying *para ter uma vida*—literally, "to have a life" in Portuguese). To measure cultural consonance in lifestyle, we simply determined the proportion of items people owned (or did, in the case of leisure activities) that were rated as at least somewhat important in defining one as being a success in life. This measure thus determines how close to the cultural prototype of lifestyle, or far from it, an individual is. Using these techniques, you can draw a straight line from natural speech acts, or, in less erudite terms, people talking about stuff, to a measurement that orders them along a continuum defined in terms of those speech acts. This is an emically valid measurement.

The payoff for developing such a measurement was demonstrated in Chapter 7. Cultural consonance in lifestyle is a better predictor of locus of control than a conventional measure of socioeconomic status. We have developed measures of cultural consonance this way in the domains of social support, family life, national identity, food, and life goals (Dressler, Borges, Balieiro, & Dos Santos 2005), and we have examined the stability over 10 years in the cultural models structuring these domains (Dressler, Balieiro, & Dos Santos 2015). Cultural consonance in these domains is associated with blood pressure (Dressler, Balieiro, Ribeiro, & Dos Santos 2005), psychological distress (Dressler 2007a), immune function (Dressler 2006), and body mass (Dressler et al. 2008, 2012). In a longitudinal study, change in cultural consonance over a two-year period was associated with change in depressive symptoms (Dressler 2007b). Finally, cultural consonance interacts with genotype to predict change in depressive symptoms over a two-year period (Dressler, Balieiro, Ribeiro, & Dos Santos 2009). We have thus documented a role of culture in health and human biology, relative to other factors widely understood to influence health outcomes, that could not have been observed without the development of an emically valid measure and the collection of quantitative data for hypothesis-testing.

This approach to measurement need not be wedded solely to the measurement of cultural consonance. A different example of this approach to measurement is the work of Gravlee and associates (Gravlee 2005; Gravlee, Dressler, & Bernard 2005; Gravlee, Non, & Mulligan 2009). Gravlee was interested in the role of cultural factors in the well-known observation that people of African descent in the Western Hemisphere tend to have higher blood pressure, and a higher prevalence of hypertension, than persons of European descent (Dressler, Oths, & Gravlee 2005). African descent can be assessed simply as skin color. The conventional view has been that this is a function of racial biology; however, the logical and empirical weakness of this explanation led to the search for other kinds of factors that could explain this difference (Dressler 1993, 2014).

Gravlee wanted to determine how race is culturally defined and to determine how taking that cultural definition into account might enter into the explanation. He chose Puerto Rico as his research site because, unlike the mainland United States, race in Puerto Rico is not considered a dichotomy; instead there are multiple descriptive terms defining skin color. Using techniques of cultural domain analysis, Gravlee elicited these terms and determined that most of them could be collapsed into three categories: *blanco* ("white"), *trigueño* ("wheat-colored"), and *negro* ("black"). Furthermore, there was cultural consensus among a sample of respondents in the allocation of persons to these categories (Gravlee 2005). In other words, there was a culturally shared model of skin color.

Next, Gravlee collected data on how observers would actually categorize a sample of 100 persons using these emically valid categories. In addition, he collected data on skin color independent of human observers (using a technique called *skin reflectance spectrophotometry*). He found that the emic categories of skin color were stronger correlates of blood pressure, in inter-action with socioeconomic status, than the "objective" reflectance measures (Gravlee et al. 2005). Finally, the emic categories of skin color were stronger correlates of blood pressure than so-called ancestry informative markers, a way of measuring genetic distance from a supposed hypothetical ancestral population (Gravlee, Dressler, & Bernard 2009). In other words, culture trumped biology.

Gravlee and associates used basically the same approach to measuring the emic categories of race as I have used in measuring cultural consonance, although I don't think we would want to say that his respondents were more or less "consonant" with the cultural model of race. Cultural consonance is a term specific to the achievement of culturally defined life goals (Dressler 2007a). But the work of Gravlee demonstrates that this approach to the development of emically valid measurements can be applied to a variety of theoretical constructs.

My main point is this: in anthropological and other ethnographic research, our aims in employing statistical analysis and integrating quantitative data into our research designs are truly anthropological goals. Yes, we are interested in statistically evaluating hypotheses, but this occurs in the context of understanding how peoples' cultural construction of the world around them influences their behavior. Getting at these cultural constructions in a way that enables us to measure theoretical constructs in an emically valid manner requires that our hypothesis-testing research be embedded in a larger ethnographic enterprise.

DISCUSSION

My aim in this chapter is to place quantification in anthropology in the larger context of the division of labor in the social sciences. Everyone adds something to the mix. My argument is that as anthropologists and ethnographers we pay much closer attention to how people construct the world around them in terms of shared meaning than other social scientific disciplines and that our mixed-methods research designs can be uniquely suited to better understanding the causal implications of those cultural constructions. Understanding cultural construction and its effects necessitates engaging in traditional ethnographic research, as well as hypothesis-testing research employing quantitative data. What links these are an intermediate set of techniques, represented here by cultural domain analysis. These research techniques transition seamlessly from purely qualitative to purely quantitative and help to clarify the continuum on which different kinds of data lie. The strength of anthropological research lies in the configuration of methods, not in the specific application of one or another method.

What I am recommending here is not without controversy. Just recently I was presenting some of my work on cultural consonance to an audience in which all major social scientific fields were represented. After my presentation an eminent sociologist and I were standing in a small group and someone made a reference to my work. The sociologist gave me a Cheshire-cat smile and said, "But what about **external validity**?"—meaning were any of my findings from this community in Brazil, emphasizing as strongly as they do local knowledge, generalizable beyond that community? Were they relevant to anywhere but Ribeirão Preto? I let the question slide with a noncommittal comment, but what I really should have said was: "Who cares?" What I mean is that if you don't have theoretical constructs and measures that are relevant to the local community, your findings are not going to be valid for that community. If you use only etic theoretical constructs and measurements, perhaps you can then compare those findings directly to those from another community, but basically what you will be comparing are two sets of findings of questionable validity for each community.

I would argue that what is much more fruitful is to have explanatory statistical models for communities that are properly specified for those communities by including emically valid theoretical constructs and measures of those constructs. Findings from various settings can still be compared, albeit qualitatively. You won't be able to directly compare the magnitude of one regression coefficient to another, but you can get a very clear idea of how these explanatory statistical models are similar or different. At this point, that's good enough.

One question that I have side-stepped somewhat is: how far do you go in making everything emically valid? A full discussion of this question is beyond the scope of this presentation; however, suffice it to say I think that it is a matter to be decided on a project-by-project basis. For example, as I write this we are collecting data in Brazil on cultural consonance and subjective well-being, the latter assessed largely by depressive symptoms. Is depressed affect a cultural universal? I think so. Does depressed affect get expressed in the same way everywhere? No, I doubt it. Should we have developed an emic measure of depressed affect in Brazil? We could have, although some data we collected on this issue indicated that a standard scale of depressive symptoms, translated and validated by other Brazilian investigators, would work well enough. Can the results from this scale be directly compared to the U.S. population? I doubt it because it seems to behave somewhat differently in Brazil; however, we have every indication that it orders people along a continuum from lower to higher expressed depressive symptoms. Just because a score of, for example, 23 on the scale in Brazil doesn't mean the same things as a score of 23 in the United States does not invalidate its use in Brazil, since a person with a score of 23 in Brazil is still communicating a lower level of subjective well-being than a person with a score of 10 in Brazil.

You can do only so much in a research project, and you have to direct your energies and resources appropriately. For us, what was most important in this project was to have emically valid measures of potential precursors of subjective well-being, so our efforts were directed in that way. All research involves these kinds of decisions.

Best of Luck!

My aim in this book has been to help interested students and colleagues think statistically. Thinking statistically can have substantial benefits in terms of clarifying our work and, indeed, clarifying our own thinking. One of the blogs that I read religiously is Paul Krugman's, the Nobel Prize-winning economist. He emphasizes the importance of having a model in his writings on economics. The point is, of course, that data do not speak for themselves. Data mean something when they are collected in terms of a theory and combined with other data using a well-specified model. The model might be wrong, but it is good to think with. It helps us to refine our thinking and direct us toward a better model.

A large part of my point is also that incorporating statistical modeling into ethnographic research is not a matter of simply including basic or even advanced statistics in our research. It is a matter of integrating quantification into our ethnographic enterprise, and especially helping us to better examine how local knowledge and understanding enter into the explanation of complex phenomena.

Anyone who has kept even a small part of their eye on anthropology over the past 25 years or so will have noticed the flailing about and teeth-gnashing going on. Anthropology as a field of study is in (or, as some optimistically put it, has gone through) a crisis, and since Marcus and Fischer (1986) famously put it this way, we might as well refer to it as a "crisis of representation." Their point was that the ethnographer, who for so long occupied a position of unquestioned authority in his or her descriptions, could no longer be granted that status. Rather, there were too many influences on the perspective of the ethnographer for him or her to be trusted as an objective observer and recorder of behavior and social organization. The solution

---

The 5 Things You Need to Know about Statistics: Quantification in Ethnographic Research by William W. Dressler, 149–151 © 2015 Left Coast Press, Inc. All rights reserved.

for Marcus and Fischer was to emphasize ethnography as, if not a literary exercise, at least a form of writing: the ethnographer as essayist. Coupled with the postmodern suspicion of "grand narratives" such as social scientific theory, the anthropological enterprise became akin to improvisation in jazz. A good jazz musician takes the theme provided by the jazz standard and then creatively plays with that theme to generate a novel solo, which can be thought of as a kind of perspective on the music. Similarly, the postmodern ethnographer takes a theme—some observation—and riffs on it until there is a finished product (meeting presentation, article, book, whatever). Issues of validity and reliability of the observations are beside the point. This is the ethnographer's perspective (see Boyer 2003 for a similar discussion).

What is striking about this is that the crisis of representation in anthropology was first identified some 15 years earlier by scientifically minded ethnographers. During the decade of the 1960s there was a lively interest in research methods in anthropology, including personal accounts of fieldwork (such as Wax 1971); specialized discussions of fieldwork techniques in the old Holt, Rinehart, and Winston series (for example, Langness 1965); and the appearance of several books on anthropological methods (Naroll & Cohen 1973; Pelto 1970). I was acutely aware of the underlying motive for the interest in research methods, since Bert Pelto was my dissertation chair in the mid-1970s. Bert's whole point in developing research methods was that the reader of an ethnography had no way of evaluating the likely validity or reliability of a statement in an ethnography. If an ethnography said that most men married their cross-cousins, what kind of confidence interval could be placed around that statement? How accurate was it? Bert's basic idea was that ethnographers needed to be more explicit about how they went about collecting their data and that they should incorporate a mix of qualitative and quantitative data in order to triangulate statements. With these modifications, readers would be in a much better position to evaluate the statements made and the confidence that could be placed in them.

Research methods in anthropology have continued to progress (witness the fact that Bernard's methods book is in its fifth edition [2011]), including the development of the cultural consensus model (Romney, Weller, & Batchelder 1986), which, in my opinion, is truly paradigmatic. The journal *Field Methods*, having evolved from *Cultural Anthropology Methods*, is thriving as a clearing-house for mixed-methods research. And as anthropologists continue to find employment outside the traditional academic environment, they find that the skills they have in doing mixed, qualitative-quantitative research are marketable.

Part of achieving this configuration of methods starts with thinking statistically. And thinking statistically starts with the 5 things you need to know about statistics (and the rest is gravy).

GLOSSARY

analysis of variance (ANOVA) Statistical technique for testing differences of means among multiple groups.

between-groups variation In analysis of variance, an estimate of variation among the groups or categories.

binary logistic regression Multiple regression technique for analyzing a dichotomous dependent variable.

bivariate Data from two variables considered simultaneously.

bivariate distribution The distribution of cases taking into account the data from two variables simultaneously.

categorical variable Variable that assigns cases to categories with either no indication of rank order among the categories or a rank order among a small number of categories.

central tendency General concept describing how cases tend to cluster around a value on a measure. This value can be used to characterize the distribution.

chi-square Statistical test of difference between two or more categorical variables.

cluster analysis Technique for identifying groups of cases or variables based on measures of similarity-dissimilarity among those cases or variables.

confidence interval An interval that can be placed around the estimate of a coefficient indicating its likely range in repeated random samples from the same population.

context of discovery In the philosophy of social science, the way in which hypotheses are generated.

context of verification In the philosophy of social science, the way in which hypotheses are evaluated.

continuous variable Variable on which a case can assume any value between its minimum and its maximum.

control variable Variables that are used to adjust for influences that are not of immediate interest in a study but that can interfere with the observation of associations of interest.

correlation coefficient Coefficient evaluating the strength of association between two variables.

correspondence analysis Technique for displaying the data from a complex cross-tabulation in two-dimensional space.

covariance Simultaneous variation in two variables. Technically, the sum formed by adding the deviations from the mean on one variable multiplied times the deviations from the mean on another variable.

cross-tabulation, 2 × 2 Table in which cases are assigned to one of four cells based on how they are simultaneously categorized on two dichotomies.

covariate Variable included in an analysis principally to control for its effects. It is usually considered a control variable not an independent variable.

cultural best estimate The answer key in cultural consensus analysis. It is the best estimate of how a culturally competent respondent will answer a set of questions.

cultural competence Estimate of respondent cultural knowledge; literally, an estimate of how well a respondent can reproduce a shared cultural model in his or her individual responses.

cultural consensus analysis Statistical model for determining the degree of sharing in responses to a fixed set of questions. Greater consensus is evidence of cultural sharing.

cultural consonance Degree to which an individual approximates, in his or her own belief and behavior, prototypes for belief and behavior encoded in shared cultural models.

cultural model Socially shared and patterned schematic or modular cognitive representation of a salient domain.

degrees of freedom Number of independent pieces of information available in a statistical test.

dependent variable The outcome of a causal process; the variable to be explained by the independent variable(s).

dichotomy Nominal variable with two categories.

distribution Array of numbers depicting the frequency with which each value of a variable appears in a sample.

dispersion General concept describing the spread of values that a variable has in a given sample.

dummy variables Set of variables created by dichotomizing each of the values of a multiple category nominal or ordinal variable. Used less frequently with continuous measures.

effects coding Assigning values of 0 and 1 to dichotomous or dummy variables.

emic perspective Research orientation in which variables that are meaningful to the population of focus form all or part of the explanatory framework of the investigator.

emic validity Degree to which a construct is a measure that is meaningful to the population of focus.

etic perspective Research orientation in which variables are meaningful in the theoretical perspective of the investigator but not necessarily to the population of focus.

explained variation The proportion of variation that can be attributed to an independent variable in a bivariate or multivariate study.

external validity The degree to which a measurement accurately assesses a variable outside the context of a specific study.

F-ratio Ratio of the between groups mean sum of squares to the within groups mean sum of squares in ANOVA; named for Sir Ronald Fisher.

factor analysis Statistical technique for identifying a reduced dimensional structure in a correlation matrix.

factorial analysis of variance Analysis of variance with more than one independent variable.

formal process model Cultural consensus model using dichotomous and multiple-choice variables.

full square symmetric matrix Matrix with the same number of rows and columns; usually refers to a correlation matrix.

hypothesis Proposition stating anticipated, testable relationships between two or more variables.

independent variable Variable that is hypothesized to influence a dependent (outcome) variable.

informal data model Cultural consensus model using continuous variables.

internal consistency Degree to which respondents answer questions in a scale in a consistent manner.

interquartile range Range of values between the 25th and 75th percentiles of a scale.

interval scale Continuous measure in which each interval on the scale is equal to every other interval on the scale.

Kruskal-Wallis one-way analysis of variance Nonparametric version, by ranks, of analysis of variance.

least-squares fit Fitting a line to data by minimizing the sum of the squared deviations of observed data points from the predicted data points that lie on the line.

linear regression Model for predicting values of a dependent variable from values of an independent variable using the equation for a straight line.

marginal In contingency table analysis the distribution of cases across the categories of a variable, displayed in the margins of the table.

mean Measure of central tendency calculated by adding all individual values of a variable for the sample and dividing by the number of cases in the sample.

median Measure of central tendency that is the value of a variable that splits the sample into two equal or near equal groups.

metric The scale of measurement of a variable.

mixed-methods research Research that integrates the collection of qualitative and quantitative data into a single research design.

mode Most frequent response on a variable (a measure of central tendency).

multiple correlation coefficient Correlation coefficient summarizing the strength of the association between one dependent and multiple independent variables.

multiple R Abbreviation for a multiple correlation coefficient.

multivariate linear regression Linear regression with a single dependent and two or more independent variables

nominal variable Variable consisting of two or more categories with no inherent order (for example, religion).

nonmetric multidimensional scaling Statistical technique that displays the pattern in a similarity/dissimilarity matrix as a set of inter-point distances in a reduced dimensional space.

nonparametric statistics Statistical tests for which there are no assumptions about the distributions of the variables.

normal distribution Univariate distribution of the values of a variable that forms a bell-shaped curve when displayed graphically.

one-way analysis of variance Statistical technique for testing the differences in means among a set of groups or categories.

ordinal variable A variable the values of which place cases in a ranked order.

parametric statistics Statistical tests based on the assumptions of random sampling and that the continuous variables used in the tests are normally distributed.

partial regression coefficient Coefficient describing the slope of the relationship between a dependent and an independent variable, while controlling for other variables.

partial correlation coefficient Coefficient describing the strength of the association between two variables, while controlling for other variables.

phi coefficient Correlation coefficient appropriate for a 2 × 2 cross-tabulation; more generally, the Pearson correlation coefficient between two dichotomous variables.

post-hoc test In analysis of variance, a test of the difference between two specific means, usually conducted only after an overall significant difference among means has been observed.

power analysis Analysis conducted to estimate the number of cases required to detect a statistically significant difference or association, given an estimate of the size of the difference.

predicted value Value of a dependent variable estimated from the value of an independent variable for each case.

protected F-test Running an overall analysis of variance before running a set of post-hoc tests.

range A measure of dispersion, calculated as the difference between the lowest and the highest values of a variable.

ratio variable Variable on which each interval is equal and there is a true zero point.

regression coefficient Coefficient that estimates the effect of an independent variable on a dependent variable. The regression coefficient is the slope of the straight line fitted to the data points.

reliability Degree to which a measure returns the same value for a case when repeated under approximately equivalent conditions.

response set Tendency for a respondent to give the same answer to a set of questions.

scatterplot Graph in which cases are plotted in space on two variables.

signal The value of a variable that would be observed if the measurement of the variable were free of all error.

simple matching coefficient A similarity coefficient calculated as the proportion of times that responses on two dichotomous variables are in agreement.

skewness Degree to which a disproportionate number of large or small values on a variable cause a distribution to depart from normality.

Spearman rank-order correlation coefficient Correlation coefficient appropriate for ordinal data.

spurious An association that is not the result of a true, underlying causal process.

standard deviation A measure of the dispersion of a normal distribution, calculated as the square root of the average deviations of cases from the mean.

standard error The standard deviation of a sampling distribution of estimated coefficients.

standardized regression coefficient Regression coefficient in which differences in measurement metric have been removed from the independent variables in the analysis.

statistical reliability An association or difference that is statistically significant; hence, it is likely to be repeated in multiple random samples drawn from the same population.

symmetric coefficient Coefficient, like the correlation coefficient, that implies no causal direction.

t-**test** Special case of the analysis of variance, when the categorical variable is a dichotomy; also known as "Student's *t*-test."

techniques of numerical induction Set of statistical techniques (factor analysis, cluster analysis, multidimensional scaling) enabling the investigator to search for underlying structure in data.

tests of association Statistical tests, such as the correlation coefficient, that assess the degree to which two variables or cases co-vary.

tests of difference Statistical tests, such as analysis of variance, that assess the degree to which two or more groups are dissimilar on one or more variables.

total variation Total amount of dissimilarity within a sample, usually assessed as the deviations of individual cases from a measure of central tendency.

unconstrained pile sort Interview technique useful for discovering the features respondents use to distinguish among a set of terms.

underlying dimension Way of conceptualizing the reduced set of parameters that characterize a similarity-dissimilarity matrix.

unexplained variation Variation in a dependent variable that cannot be allocated to an independent variable.

univariate distribution Characterizing the distribution of a set of cases on a single variable.

variance Estimate of dispersion: the average of the squared deviations of cases from the mean of a distribution. Variance is the standard deviation squared.

within-groups variation In analysis of variance, the variation within identified groups or categories that is left unaccounted for by the independent variable.

z-**score** Score formed by subtracting the mean from the value of a variable for each case and then dividing by the standard deviation.

REFERENCES

Berkman, L. F., & Kawachi, I. (Eds.). (2000). *Social Epidemiology*. New York: Oxford University Press.

Bernard, H. R. (2011). *Research Methods in Anthropology* (5th ed.). Walnut Creek, CA: AltaMira Press.

Bernard, H. R., & Ryan, G. W. (2010) *Analyzing Qualitative Data: Systematic Approaches*. Thousand Oaks, CA: Sage Publications.

Bhaskar, R. (1989). *Reclaiming Reality: A Critical Introduction to Contemporary Philosophy*. London: Verso.

Blalock, H. M., Jr. (1960). *Social Statistics*. New York: McGraw-Hill.

Borgatti, S. P. (1994). Cultural domain analysis. *Journal of Quantitative Anthropology, 4*(4), 261–78.

_____. (1999). Elicitation techniques for cultural domain analysis. In J. J. Schensul, M. D. LeCompte, B. K. Nastasi, and S. P. Borgatti (Eds.), *Ethnographer's Toolkit: Enhanced Ethnographic Methods*, Vol. 3 (pp. 115–51). Walnut Creek, CA: AltaMira Press.

Bourdieu, P. (1984). *Distinction: A Social Critique of the Judgment of Taste*. Cambridge, MA: Harvard University Press.

Boyer, P. (2003). Science, erudition and relevant connections. *Journal of Cognition and Culture, 3*(4), 344–58.

Carneiro, R. L. (1962). Scale analysis as an instrument for the study of cultural evolution. *Southwestern Journal of Anthropology, 18*, 149–69.

Cohen, J., & Cohen, P. (1975). *Applied Multiple Regression/Correlation Analysis for the Behavioral Sciences*. Hillsdale, NJ: Lawrence Erlbaum Associates.

Coreil, J., & Marsall, P. (1982). Locus of illness control: A cross-cultural study. *Human Organization, 41*, 131–38.

DeWalt, K. M., & DeWalt, B. R. (2011). *Participant Observation: A Guide for Fieldworkers*. Lanham, MD: AltaMira Press.

Dressler, W. (1979). "Disorganization," adaptation, and arterial blood pressure. *Medical Anthropology, 3*, 225–48.

_____. (1980). Ethnomedical beliefs and patient adherence to a treatment regimen: A St. Lucian example. *Human Organization, 39*, 88–91.

_____. (1982). *Hypertension and Culture Change: Acculturation and Disease in the West Indies*. South Salem, NY: Redgrave Publishing.

_____. (1985). Psychosomatic symptoms, stress and modernization: A model. *Culture, Medicine, and Psychiatry, 9*(3), 257–86.

_____. (1990). Lifestyle, stress, and blood pressure in a Southern black community. *Psychosomatic Medicine, 52*(2), 182–98.

_____. (1993). Health in the African American community: Accounting for health inequalities. *Medical Anthropology Quarterly, 7*(4), 325–45.

_____. (1994). Cross-cultural differences and social influences in social support and cardiovascular disease. In S. A. Shumaker & S. M. Czajkowski (Eds.), *Social Support and Cardiovascular Disease* (pp. 167–92). New York: Plenum Publishing.

_____. (1995). Modeling biocultural interactions: Examples from studies of stress and cardiovascular disease. *Yearbook of Physical Anthropology, 38*, 27–56.

_____. (1996). Using cultural consensus analysis to develop a measurement: A Brazilian example. *Cultural Anthropology Methods, 8*, 6–8.

_____. (1995). Modeling biocultural interactions: Examples from studies of stress and cardiovascular disease." *Yearbook of Physical Anthropology 38*: 27–56.

_____. (2001). Medical anthropology: Toward a third moment in social science? *Medical Anthropology Quarterly, 15*(4), 455–65.

_____. (2005). What's *cultural* about bio*cultural* research? *Ethos, 33*(1), 20–45.

_____. (2006) Cultural consonance and c-reactive protein in urban Brazil. *Abstracts of the 105th Annual Meeting of the American Anthropological Association*, Nov. 15–19, San Jose, CA.

_____. (2007a). Cultural consonance. In D. Bhugra & K. Bhui (Eds.), *Textbook of Cultural Psychiatry* (pp. 179–90). New York: Cambridge University Press.

_____. (2007b). Meaning and structure in research in medical anthropology. *Anthropology in Action, 14*(3), 30–43.

_____. (2014). Race and public health. In W. C. Cockerham, R. Dingwall, & S. Quah (Eds.), *The Wiley Blackwell Encyclopedia of Health, Illness, Behavior, and Society* (pp. 2017–21). Chichester: John Wiley & Sons, Ltd.

Dressler, W., Balieiro, M., & Dos Santos, J. (1997). The cultural construction of social support in Brazil: Associations with health outcomes. *Culture, Medicine, and Psychiatry, 21*(3), 303–35.

_____. (1998). Culture, socioeconomic status, and physical and mental health in Brazil. *Medical Anthropology Quarterly, 12*(4), 424–46.

_____. (2002). Cultural consonance and psychological distress. *Paidéia: Cadernos de Psicologia e Educação, 12*, 5–18.

_____. (2015). Finding culture in the second factor: Stability and change in cultural consensus and residual agreement. *Field Methods, 27*(1).

Dressler, W., Balieiro, M., Ribeiro, R., & Dos Santos, J. (2005). Cultural consonance and arterial blood pressure in urban Brazil. *Social Science & Medicine, 61*(3), 527–40.

_____. (2007a). Cultural consonance and psychological distress: Examining the associations in multiple cultural domains. *Culture, Medicine, and Psychiatry, 31*(2), 195–224.

_____. (2007b). A prospective study of cultural consonance and depressive symptoms in urban Brazil. *Social Science & Medicine, 65*(10), 2058–69.

_____. (2009). Cultural consonance, a 5HT2A receptor polymorphism, and depressive symptoms: A longitudinal study of gene x culture interaction in urban Brazil. *American Journal of Human Biology, 21*(1), 91–97.

Dressler, W., & Bindon, J. (2000). The health consequences of cultural consonance: Cultural dimensions of lifestyle, social support, and arterial blood pressure in an African American community. *American Anthropologist, 102*(2), 244–60.

Dressler, W., Borges, C. D., Balieiro, M. C., & Dos Santos, J. E. (2005). Measuring cultural consonance: Examples with special reference to measurement theory in anthropology. *Field Methods, 17*(4), 331–55.

Dressler, W., Dos Santos, J., & Balieiro, M. (1996). Studying diversity and sharing in culture: An example of lifestyle in Brazil. *Journal of Anthropological Research, 52*(3), 331–53.

Dressler, W., Dos Santos, J., Gallagher, P., & Viteri, F. (1987). Arterial blood pressure and modernization in Brazil. *American Anthropologist, 89*(2), 398–409.

Dressler, W., Grell, G., & Viteri, F. (1995). Intracultural diversity and the sociocultural correlates of blood pressure: A Jamaican example. *Medical Anthropology Quarterly, 9*(3), 291–313.

Dressler, W., Mata, A., Chavez, A., & Viteri, F. (1987). Arterial blood pressure and individual modernization in a Mexican community. *Social Science & Medicine, 24*(8), 679–87.

Dressler, W., & Oths, K. S. (2014). Social survey methods. In H. R. Bernard & C. C. Gravlee (Eds.), *Handbook of Methods in Cultural Anthropology* (2nd ed.). Lanham, MD: AltaMira Press.

Dressler, W., Oths, K. S., Balieiro, M. C., Ribeiro, R. P., & Dos Santos, J. E. (2012). How culture shapes the body: Cultural consonance and body mass in urban Brazil. *American Journal of Human Biology, 24*(3), 325–31.

Dressler, W., Oths, K. S., & Gravlee, C. (2005). Race and ethnicity in public health research: Models to explain health disparities. *Annual Review of Anthropology, 34,* 231–52.

Dressler, W., Oths, K. S., Ribeiro, R. P., Balieiro, M. C., & Dos Santos, J. E. (2008). Cultural consonance and adult body composition in urban Brazil. *American Journal of Human Biology, 20*(1), 15–22.

Ember, C. R., & Ember, M. (2009). *Cross-Cultural Research Methods* (2nd ed.). Lanham, MD: AltaMira Press.

Fidler, F., Thomason, N., Cumming, G., Finch, S., & Leeman, J. (2004). Editors can lead researchers to confidence intervals, but can't make them think: Statistical reform lessons from medicine. *Psychological Science, 15*(2), 119–26.

Fisher, R. A. (1925). *Statistical Methods for Research Workers.* Edinburgh: Oliver and Boyd.

Goodenough, W. (1996). Culture. In D. Levinson and M. Ember (Eds.), *Encyclopedia of Cultural Anthropology* (pp. 291–99). New York: Henry Holt.

Goodman, L. A. (1969). How to ransack social mobility tables and other kinds of cross-classification tables. *American Journal of Sociology, 75*(1), 1–40.

Gravlee, C. C. (2005). Ethnic classification in southeastern Puerto Rico: The cultural model of color. *Social Forces, 83*(3), 949–70.

Gravlee, C. C., Dressler, W., & Bernard, H. (2005). Skin color, social classification, and blood pressure in southeastern Puerto Rico. *American Journal of Public Health, 95*(12), 2191–97.

Gravlee, C. C., Non, A. L., & Mulligan, C. J. (2009). Genetic ancestry, social classification, and racial inequalities in blood pressure in southeastern Puerto Rico. *PLoS ONE, 4*(9), e6821.

Handwerker, W. P., & Borgatti, S. P. (2014). Reasoning with numbers. In H. R. Bernard & C. C. Gravlee (Eds.), *Handbook of Methods in Cultural Anthropology* (2nd ed.). Lanham, MD: AltaMira Press.

Henry, J. P., & Cassel, J. C. (1969). Psychosocial factors in essential hypertension. Recent epidemiologic and animal experimental evidence. *American Journal of Epidemiology, 90*(3), 171–200.

Janes, C. (1990). *Migration, Social Change, and Health: A Samoan Community in Urban California.* Stanford: Stanford University Press.

Kessler, R. C., & Neighbors, H. W. (1986). A new perspective on the relationships among race, social class, and psychological distress. *Journal of Health and Social Behavior, 27*(2), 107–15.

Kroeber, A. L. (1917). The superorganic. *American Anthropologist, 19*(2), 163–213.

Langness, L. L. (1965). *The Life History in Anthropological Science.* New York: Holt, Rinehart and Winston.

Lazarus, R. S. (1966). *Psychological Stress and the Coping Process.* New York: McGraw-Hill.

Malinowski, B. (1961). *Argonauts of the Western Pacific.* New York: E.P. Dutton. (Original published in 1922)

Marcus, G. E., & Fischer, M. M. J. (1986). *Anthropology as Cultural Critique: An Experimental Moment in the Human Sciences.* Chicago: University of Chicago Press.

Mlodinow, L. (2009). *The Drunkard's Walk: How Randomness Rules Our Lives.* New York: Vintage.

Moore, J. D. (2012). *Visions of Culture: An Introduction to Anthropological Theories and Theorists* (4th ed.). Lanham, MD: AltaMira Press.

Murdock, G. P. (1940). The cross-cultural survey. *American Sociological Review, 5*(3): 361–70.

Naroll, R., & Cohen, R. (1973). *Handbook of Method in Cultural Anthropology.* New York: Columbia University Press.

Oths, K. S., Dunn, L. L., & Palmer, N. S. (2001). A prospective study of psychosocial job strain and birth outcomes. *Epidemiology, 12*(6), 744–46.

Pelto, P. J. (1970). *Anthropological Research: The Structure of Inquiry.* New York: Harper & Row.

Pelto, P. J., & Pelto, G. H. (1975). Intra-cultural diversity: Some theoretical issues. *American Ethnologist, 2*(1), 1–18.

_____. (1978). *Anthropological Research: The Structure of Inquiry* (2nd ed.). New York: Cambridge University Press.

Phillips, J. L. J. (1981). *Statistical Thinking: A Structural Approach* (2nd ed.). San Francisco: W. H. Freeman & Company.

Pike, K. L. (1954). *Language in Relation to a Unified Theory of the Structure of Human Behavior* (Vol. 1). Glendale, CA: Summer Institute of Linguistics.

Romney, A. K., Weller, S. C., & Batchelder, W. H. (1986). Culture as consensus: A theory of culture and informant accuracy. *American Anthropologist, 88*(2), 313–38.

Rotter, J. B. (1990). Internal versus external control of reinforcement: A case history of a variable. *American Psychologist, 45*(4), 489–93.

Rudner, R. S. (1966). *Philosophy of Social Science.* Englewood Cliffs, NJ: Prentice-Hall.

Smith, M. G. (1962). *West Indian Family Structure.* Seattle: University of Washington Press.

Smith, R. T. (1971). Culture and social structure in the Caribbean. In *Peoples and Cultures of the Caribbean.* Garden City, NY: Natural History Press.

Stevens, S. S. (1946). On the theory of scales of measurement. *Science, 103*(2684), 677–80.

Veblen, T. (1912). *The Theory of the Leisure Class* (new ed.). New York: The Macmillan Company.

Wax, R. H. (1971). *Doing Fieldwork: Warnings and Advice.* Chicago, IL: University of Chicago Press.

Weller, S. C. (2007). Cultural consensus theory: Applications and frequently asked questions. *Field Methods, 19*(4), 339–68.

_____. (2015). Sample size estimation: The easy way. *Field Methods 27.*

Weller, S. C., & Romney, A. K. (1988). *Systematic Data Collection.* Newbury Park, CA: Sage Publications.

Whitt, H. P. (1983). Status inconsistency: A body of negative evidence or a statistical artifact? *Social Forces, 62*(1), 201–30.

INDEX

ABOUT THE AUTHOR

William W. Dressler, professor of anthropology at the University of Alabama, is a medical anthropologist with interests in culture theory, community studies, research methods, and the relationship between culture and disease. He has adapted models of psychosocial stress to examine the association between social and cultural factors and the risk of chronic disease, including cardiovascular disease. His recent work emphasizes concepts and methods needed to evaluate the health effects of individual efforts to achieve culturally defined goals and aspirations, and he has helped develop research methods for the study of connections among cultural, individual, and biological spheres. His research has been conducted in settings as diverse as urban Great Britain, the southeast United States, the West Indies, Mexico, and Samoa.